PELICAN BOOKS

A679

UNITED NATIONS:
PIETY, MYTH, AND TRUTH

ANDREW BOYD

Andrew Boyd was born in 1920 and educated at Winchester and Oxford. In the Second World War he spent six years in the army and served with the Fourteenth Army on the Burma front. In 1946 he was a British liaison officer with delegates attending the first session of the United Nations Assembly in London. That year he published *The United Nations Organisation Handbook*, the first book on the subject to be published in Britain. From 1947 to 1950 he worked for the British U.N. Association, and since 1951 he has been on the editorial staff of *The Economist*, for which he writes on international affairs. He has travelled widely and attended a number of major international conferences, visiting the U.N. Headquarters in New York several times. His other books include *An Atlas of World Affairs* (1957), which has gone into five editions. Andrew Boyd, who lives in London, is married to a former editor of the journal of the U.N. Association.

ANDREW BOYD

*

UNITED NATIONS

Piety, Myth, and Truth

Penguin Books

BALTIMORE · MARYLAND

Penguin Books Ltd, Harmondsworth, Middlesex, England
Penguin Books Inc., 3300 Clipper Mill Road, Baltimore 11, Md, u.s.a.
Penguin Books Pty Ltd, Ringwood
Victoria, Australia

—

First published as a Penguin Special 1962
Revised edition published in Pelican Books 1964

—

Copyright © Andrew Boyd, 1962, 1964

—

Made and printed in Great Britain
by C. Nicholls & Company Ltd
Set in Monotype Baskerville

Contents

Preface

IT is better that people should argue about the United Nations, however heatedly, than that it should be paid lip-service and politely shelved, as has been the case too often in the past. But fruitful argument needs to be based on an understanding of what the UN really is.

This book seeks to explain some essential realities of the organization. It does not, therefore, set out the complex structure of the UN's many committees and other organs. Nor does it linger on the outward form of public debate and procedure. Instead it looks behind the scene, at developments that are often only dimly perceived. Its concentration on the UN's political aspects is not meant to suggest that the organization's economic and social work is unimportant.

For brevity's sake, the Security Council is often referred to in these pages simply as the Council. No disrespect is intended to the Economic and Social Council or to the Trusteeship Council; it is simply that this is, as I have said, a political book.

Apologies for other brevities: 'Britain', in this book, frequently means Her Majesty's Government in the United Kingdom of Great Britain and Northern Ireland; 'Russia', the government of the Union of Soviet Socialist Republics; a citizen of the United Arab Republic may be described as an Egyptian; and so on. This kind of shorthand, however necessary if one is trying to write readably, is, unfortunately, liable to be most misleading in the case of the United Nations itself. Strictly, the UN ought hardly ever to be mentioned without a qualifying word or phrase to make clear that one is talking about the Assembly, the Secretariat, the body of member nations, or whatever.

Apologies to those who dislike the name of Turtle Bay. The location of UN headquarters needs some shorthand term, and 'New York' does not indicate what one is

referring to as readily as, say, 'Geneva' used to indicate
the League of Nations. Turtlophobes can rest assured that I
would not venture to offend them except under compelling
necessity; their formidable power as a 'lobby' is evident in
the fact that they have managed to keep many people convinced that the UN is still at Lake Success, which it evacuated
in 1952.

Apologies to all who may be put out at finding themselves,
or not finding themselves, in these pages.

Apologies – and warm thanks – to all who have borne
with me patiently and helped me greatly during the writing
of this book. As some of them (for respectable reasons)
would prefer not to be mentioned, it seems best to mention
no one except my wife, who has had to show the greatest
patience and has given the most help. The responsibility
for all expressions of opinion – and for any errors – is mine.
The credit for the fact that the book has been written at all
is hers.

A.B.

1 · One World in Two Minds

A SICKLY baby is a distressing sight. The perils of early childhood once past, however, a muscular adolescent can arouse a different kind of alarm. We like children to grow to manhood; but we do not always like what they do with their grown strength. Some such thoughts must spring to the mind of anybody who contrasts the judgements commonly passed on the United Nations in its infancy with those that have circulated in recent years.

A scathing chorus of Press comment greeted, for instance, the opening of the 1947 UN Assembly. It was dismissed as 'a mere debating society' which 'only stirs up trouble', and as 'no more than a platform for communist propaganda' (the Communist Press was equally busy denouncing it as an 'American-dominated mechanism for deceiving the world's peoples'). Derision was the common chord struck, in these early days, by the *Daily Mirror* ('We're not interested in the comic cuts organization'), by the *Wall Street Journal* ('degenerated from a useless debating society to a mutual vilification society') and by the *Catholic Herald* ('Every honest and realist person knows in his heart that the United Nations is dead').

How times have changed. 'Dead' within two years of its birth in 1945, the UN nevertheless survived (or should one say it was resurrected or reincarnated?) to enter the 1960s with unexpected vigour. True, General de Gaulle has dismissed '*les nations dites unies*' as nothing more than a '*machin*' (a what d'you call it). But the French President has been almost alone in the disdain department. Lately, the UN's sharpest critics have seemed to see it not as a mewling infant but as a kind of razor gang. Fairly typical of this more respectful (in one sense) approach was the grim vision that the *Sunday Telegraph* conjured up, in December 1961, of a Secretariat that has tasted blood. . . . There can be no doubt that the UN Secretariat now has the bit between its teeth, and nothing short of a deliberate check by the Western powers will prevent it from galloping away to disaster.

By then the weakling child had been transformed, according to Lord Hinchingbrooke,* writing in the *Sunday Express,* into 'a charging rhinoceros, tearing up the earth', a 'monster of iniquity', a 'juggernaut which is rolling down upon us'. The then Conservative M.P. for South Dorset went on to serve warning that

the more the United Nations is groomed to refinement and maturity, the more potent for evil it may become ... now, when contingents of troops from all over the world are rallying under its banner, apprehension steadily grows. . . . The United Nations is fast becoming Britain's principal enemy. We may have to mobilize support from wherever we can to defeat it, if we and our Commonwealth are to survive.

Less shrill, but recognizably in the same cadence, were the notes of alarm sounded in a famous speech at Berwick in December 1961 by the then British Foreign Secretary in person. Lord Home declared that there was 'a crisis of confidence in the United Nations'. He made it clear that it was not any sign of helpless passivity on the UN's part that now troubled him. It was just the opposite: the UN had become altogether too disturbingly active. Its Assembly was 'persistently' passing resolutions that 'can only be described as reckless and careless of peace'. A stage had been reached, he said,

when a large part of the organization which is dedicated to peace openly condones aggression; when an organization which was founded to sustain law and order encourages policies which must endanger it. . . . This evidence of a serious falling away from the principles of the Charter places Britain in an appalling dilemma.

Just two weeks before that, Mr Macmillan, then Prime Minister, had himself told the House of Commons that

*Who has since become Lord Sandwich.

what is so terrible is the fact that this peaceful instrument of the United Nations is not preventing civil war. This is a battle between the United Nations and the Katanga people.... I fear that we may find the United Nations slipping into a war of conquest. That is not their mandate, and not their business.

Thus, it would seem, the sickly baby had emerged, at what should have been the sweet age of seventeen, as a conquering juggernaut, or at least a kind of Frankenstein monster. It is ironic to recall how many of those who stood round the cradle in 1945 expressed the godmotherly wish that the UN, in contrast to the weakness of the pre-war League of Nations, should be 'a League with teeth'. Once it had grown a few teeth, and used them, the cry went up that its bite was worse than its former toothless bark.

Even more ironic, in its way, was the basic unity in alarm at this trend between the British and Soviet governments. This unity was concealed beneath the superficial pattern of the two governments' attitudes to specific UN questions. On the surface, it was their differences that caught the eye. In Katanga, Britain sought to stay the UN's hand, while Russia clamoured for bold action. (On the other hand, Russia refused to share the costs of the operations in the Congo for which it had voted, while Britain, which had abstained in that vote, duly paid its share.) Britain has defended the principle of the impartiality of the Secretariat against the Soviet attempt to destroy it by introducing the 'troika' system. Lord Home has hoped to get 'back to working the Charter as it was meant to be'; Mr Khrushchev wants to revise it drastically. (In both cases, there has thus been an intriguing reversal of former positions.)

At bottom, however, the two governments have revealed similar attitudes. Both sought to restore the eroded privileges of the great powers in the UN. Both were alarmed by the unexpectedly vigorous activity in the UN of the independent-minded states whose ranks have been swollen by new admissions, and whose influence in both Assembly and Secretariat has grown as the role of the Security Council has dwindled. Both have been frightened by the 'charging rhinoceros' – by discovering that the UN has acquired an unforeseen executive that is sometimes capable of acting against the wishes of one or more of the major powers. Both would have liked to hamstring this insolent animal.

There is nothing surprising about the fact of both governments insisting that they are devoted to the cause of the UN, and that their aim is to make it more effective, not less. Neither claim is necessarily altogether insincere. It just happens that London and Moscow have lately been two places where one can observe most clearly a state of mind which the mere existence of the UN evokes almost everywhere – a state of political schizophrenia.

Most people, and virtually all governments, are split-minded about the United Nations. This is natural enough. On the one hand, experience of the pains and perils of modern international anarchy has created, not only among political sophisticates but also among millions of plain sensible people, a strong wish to transform that anarchy into an ordered world. On the other hand, ours is a nationalist age. 'We, the peoples', as the preamble to the UN Charter says, may well be 'determined to save succeeding generations from the scourge of war'. But 'we, the peoples' are not at all keen about getting pushed around by a lot of foreigners. And, whatever your nationality, most of the other members of the human race are foreigners.

Governments are, equally naturally, even more split-minded about the UN than the average individual. They are more directly involved. The UN is – more precisely, was – their creation. Collectively, they shape its policies, or at least rough-hew them. They are responsible for its very existence, which they could terminate by joint action at any moment. But a national government, by definition, itself exists to serve a national interest. It may do this job wisely or short-sightedly, conscientiously or cynically; the fact remains that that is the job it is supposed to do. Many governments have been brought down when their domestic opponents could brand them as having failed to defend the country's interests; no government ever fell from power

merely because it wagged the flag proudly. Thus the very
nature of national governments makes it hard for them to
let the UN curb their sovereignty.

<u>Panic, however, is a great solvent.</u> Given a healthy scare,
people and even governments sometimes lose their normal
inhibitions for long enough to take at least one step in the
direction of world order. The UN, like the League before
it, was originally set up by governments that had undergone the shock of world war. Its remarkable subsequent
development can be directly related to a series of crises and
conflicts, each of which has enlarged its role.

It is often said, and sometimes perhaps believed, that the
UN would have worked much more effectively if the post-
war years had not been years of such stress and strain. But
it is also possible that a long spell of political calm might
have completely stunted its growth. Anxiety is frequently
expressed at the danger of overloading the organization.
True, it may yet crack under some future strain; but it has
already survived strains which were supposedly lethal. Perhaps there is no need to worry about the danger of under-
loading, of starving the UN of the troubles that have
turned out to be such invigorating baby-food. That kind of
diet will no doubt always be available.

Trouble, after all, is the UN's business. Even those who
hold that it should be limited to a role as 'a centre for
harmonizing the actions of nations' are implicitly assuming
that the job starts from disharmony. Of Dag Hammarskjöld,
the master practitioner of more vigorous UN action, some
disgruntled unknown once said: 'Wherever that man goes,
there's trouble.'

Tackling the troubles of a split-minded world is a sure
way of running into trouble oneself. Is it imaginable that
the UN could escape criticism, from one quarter or another
(and sometimes from several quarters at the same time), once
it takes a hand in any conflict of interest? A Secretariat
official newly returned from the Congo, battered (physically
as well as morally) but still willing, put the point in three
rueful words: 'You can't win.'

In each separate situation, this is true: the UN can't win. The more extended its role, the more it is exposed to censure. But the long term is another matter. Already there have been cases of member states violently opposing an extension of the UN's role in particular circumstances, being overridden, and later quietly accepting the accomplished fact, in some instances even appealing to the precedent that had been set against their wishes.

Nor is the chorus of criticism necessarily going to swell ever louder as the UN gains ground. In time, the organization may be more clearly seen for what it really is. That should dispose of a good deal of the kind of criticism that it has encountered; for much of this arises from wildly mistaken notions of its present nature and future prospects.

So powerful and prevalent are these myths that they had best be noted and dissected before we go any further.

2 · *Mysticism and Nonsense*

GOOD OLD MUM

THE most naïve of the major illusions about the UN is one that aptly lends itself to being described in childlike terms. It is the myth of a miraculous mother-figure.

As any child knows, Mum is there to provide you with whatever you feel like asking for at any given moment. It is her job to guarantee you shelter and sustenance whether you are being well behaved or naughty; and, stray as you may, always to be there when you eventually come home. Mum comforts and protects you when you run to her, squealing, after a fight you ought not really to have got into. But, as a self-respecting child, you naturally resist her attempts to impose discipline.

If you get caught snatching another child's toys, you count on Mum's indulgence. If she says she is losing patience with you altogether, and that if you don't mend your ways she will leave you to get on without her, you know she is just bluffing. Mum can't quit.

This fairly describes the underlying attitude of those who assume that an international organization should be able to give every state a full measure of aid and protection, to help it gain its particular aspirations – but should not in any way inhibit its carefree enjoyment of sovereign irresponsibility. It goes without saying that no organization whose members thus simultaneously exploit and flout it can endure. One day the spoilt child finds that Mum just isn't there any more, and the world is cold and hard and lonely.

States are sometimes slower to learn this lesson than children. One might have thought that the painful experience of the League period would have brought it home at least to those nations that felt most directly the grim consequences of their own error in giving the League too little and asking too much. Yet even they were not completely cured. The tendency to count on the UN to give out what was never put into it is not found only among inexperienced 'new nations'.

The record of 1947-9 in Palestine is an instructive example. The Arab states alternated between clamouring for the UN to satisfy their demands, and rejecting its appeals. Britain dumped the whole Palestine problem in the UN's lap but was reluctant to see the UN properly equipped to handle the job. America and Russia both bear responsibility for pushing the 1947 partition plan through an unhappy Assembly while likewise making no serious effort to equip the UN to carry it out.

The Congo has provided fresh examples of member states coupling extravagant demands on the UN with refusal to contribute toward its efforts, or to accept the policy determined for it by consensus. But childlike innocence does not account for all of these cases. Russia, for instance, has never paid a copeck towards the Congo operation – for which it has both voted and expressed fervent lip-service support at times, although at other times it has veered wildly between demanding that the UN quit the Congo altogether and pressing for it to take more ambitious (and more costly) action there. One would hesitate to class this as a simple case of Mum-fixation.

One point should be cleared up here. Recent statements by British ministers have given the impression that the UN's Asian and African members were laggard contributors, while the founder members of 1945 were conscientious in paying all their dues. The facts are quite different. When the UN faced bankruptcy in 1962, the regrettably small number of states that had paid up all their obligations, including the special levies for the Congo and for the international force on the Egypt-Israel border (UNEF), included Burma, Cameroon, Ceylon, Chad, Cyprus, India, Ivory Coast, Japan, Liberia, Malaya, Nigeria, Senegal, Thailand, and Tunisia. Many founder members had made a worse showing. The worst laggards, those over a year behind with their basic dues, numbered thirteen; of these, ten – Nationalist China, Argentina, and eight smaller Latin-American republics – were founder members.

THE SAINTS HAVE COME MARCHING IN

More sophisticated than the infantile myth about the UN – and thus more productive of confusion – is the idealizing myth. It is apt to lurk (as, indeed, do the other myths) a little below the level of consciousness.

Few people, if asked, would claim to believe that the UN has already brought the world the blessings of the rule of the saints. Yet many reactions to particular events suggest this underlying belief. Behind such remarks as 'The UN ought to have dealt with that long ago', or 'I'd never have expected the UN to stoop to horse-trading', there is often an unstated assumption that the organization already wields the power of an irresistible world government – and that the ministers in this government are ministering angels.

Many people were led to think that the mere establishment of the UN (like that of the League a generation earlier) meant an end of power politics. Both League and UN were born at the weary end of frightful wars. Both naturally attracted much of the idealizing emotion that welled up among masses of people as the nightmare faded into what seemed a new dawn. Commentators in America have come to deplore, in particular, the fact that the UN was 'sold' to many of their people as a neat and glossy 'package'. Keener eyes saw through the gift wrapping from the start, and knew that the real contents were a do-it-yourself kit – with incomplete instructions and a price tag. Others have not fully faced this painful discovery yet.

Belief that the UN was a device strong enough to shield any country from attack took a heavy pounding in its first years. But this belief was still widespread in 1949, when the governments that then formed the Atlantic alliance were accused of 'bypassing' the UN instead of relying on it for security. In 1956 the subliminal notion of an all-powerful machine produced angry charges that only a 'double standard' which rated Suez above Budapest had prevented the UN from rescuing Hungary from the Soviet Army – without risk of world war. Again, in 1962, when the two great nuclear powers jarred together over Cuba, many people seemed shaken to 'discover' that the UN was 'powerless' to halt them.

<u>Illusion breeds disillusion.</u> The recurring question, 'What's the good of the United Nations if it can't ... defend x, repulse y, achieve z?' expresses the idealizers' bitterness each time they are brusquely reminded that it can't. In 1961 the question was shrilly asked by some when India took over Goa from Portugal; by others when Patrice Lumumba was murdered in the Congo. Those who voiced it in the first case skated over the delicate fact that a Soviet veto had saved Britain and other countries from the nasty possibility of having to try to reimpose Dr Salazar's rule in Goa by force. The second lot of questioners skated over the fact that Lumumba fell into his enemies' hands only when he rashly (or on evil advice) abandoned the protection against them that UN troops had been giving him for months, and that, thereafter, the UN could probably not have rescued him alive even if it had then had the necessary authority and consent to fight a bloody battle for this purpose.

Bloodshed is not, of course, normally associated with the rule of the saints. So it is natural that the myth of UN almightiness often goes with the <u>belief that the UN ought somehow to be able to gain all its ends by moral force alone.</u> The massive and bitter three-year campaign in Korea did not destroy this belief (Korea has, admittedly, come to be regarded as a misleading phase in UN evolution; see page 97). In 1961 the belief in irresistible morality worked so powerfully on the British government that it could claim to want the immediate ejection of Tshombe's mercenaries while insisting that they must not be actually ejected. Many less sophisticated people were simply shaken, at the time of the Katanga fighting, by seeing a 'peace force' in combat.

Had not a thin blue-bereted line of UN troops steadied the

Egypt–Israel frontier for five years, strong because its heart was pure and because at its back stood the 'conscience of the world'? The idea that a UN soldier should need no weapon more lethal than a blue flag on a pole is an attractive one. To *hope* that duty will never require such a soldier to kill, even in defensive action, one does not need to be an idealizer. To *assume* this, however, is something else.

In real life moral force has, regrettably, limitations. It might be enough to secure the goals of a UN directed by beings of superhuman virtue. But in real life the UN is a political institution, run by people. Often its policy must represent an untidy compromise, reached after tedious haggling; a compromise shaped not by the dispassionate play of fine judicial minds, but by the balance of political forces at the time. The Charter itself is such a compromise, achieved by such haggling, shaped by such a balance of forces.

Here again the idealizer's illusion can breed bitter disillusion. But who could seriously have supposed that, merely by coming together at UN meetings, the representatives of wrangling (and sometimes wily) governments would at once be purified and cast aside old habits? Archangels are simply not available. Political institutions on the international level, as on the national and the parish-pump levels, are operated by people – and by people accustomed to getting results by what one man will describe as skilful negotiation, his opponent as 'intrigue' or 'manoeuvres'.

Speeches at UN meetings certainly often (too often) include protestations of devotion to high ideals. So do the speeches that politicians of all countries make on their home ground. This ancient custom has one or two useful and practical aspects. But a politician who practises what he thus preaches so literally that he never haggles, never compromises on the possible instead of vainly demanding the perfect, and never builds up support for his pet projects by 'horse-trading' is soon out of politics. This is fully as true of Communist and other authoritarian systems as of democratic ones. It is also, visibly, true of politicking in the UN.

Just as in political life at home, the public has to learn to distinguish realities from pieties in UN politics. For a start, one might suggest a quick look at the word 'peace-loving', a widely self-applied label. The Charter stipulates that only peace-loving states may join the organization. The fifty-one states which were qualified in 1945 to become founder members of the UN were so qualified by virtue of the fact that they were all at war.

This is not to say that the whole UN enterprise is a piece of humbug run by hypocrites. But the idealizer must be thrust firmly aside if the UN is to be seen clearly for what it is: a human institution marked by a familiar human blend of sincerity and deception and self-deception.

Medieval villagers went to church to trade as well as to pray. So, too, delegates are apt to sit through the rhetorical pieties of an Assembly session, calculating what worth-while deals they can make for their own countries, studying the state of the political market, and, even while an orator is pronouncing the most solemn incantations, getting down to discreet chaffering by twos and threes in corners. Each of them in due course makes his own ritual genuflexion in debate; but this should not lead anyone to think that he has come to surrender all his possessions, or to embark on a new and selfless life.

If the UN were to be strictly classified as a holy place, and the horse-traders scourged out of the temple, they would merely resume their haggling somewhere else. No new congregation of superior virtue would appear to fill their vacated places; and such opportunities as their coming together provides for the spread of enlightenment about self-interest would be lost. The UN, in fact, has to be run with people as they are, in the hope – a not unfounded hope – that the understanding of the common interests of nations will improve as association and cooperation become habit-forming. It is no good simply bewailing the discovery that a race of saints has yet to be born.

NOTHING BUT THE BEST

There are those who, while under no illusion that the UN already represents the rule of the saints, nevertheless assume that some day, somehow, there can be a spectacular breakthrough to a new and ordered world. It follows from this assumption that it is useless, indeed dangerous, to mess about trying to use the UN in its present imperfect state, because the doubtfully good is the enemy of the best.

This perfectionist myth now seems to infect some practising and prominent politicians as well as some ardent crusaders for world government. Or, if the infection has two different origins, the symptoms come out remarkably alike.

Several authors of impressive blue prints for world government have accompanied them with very logical attacks on the illogicality and imperfections of the UN mechanism. It would be foolish to try to defend the UN against such critics by making it out to be more than it is. It neither is nor pretends to be a world government – although as cautious an observer as Walter Lippmann, America's most distinguished columnist, has remarked that 'The world state is inherent in the United Nations, as an oak tree is in an acorn.'

The UN is not satisfactorily representative of the peoples of the world according to any really democratic formula. Its authority has often been defied by great powers and small alike. The Charter makes no claim to abolish the separate sovereignties of the nations. Its Article 2 contains the famous paragraph (7), which formally prohibits UN intervention in 'matters which are essentially within the domestic jurisdiction of any state'.

The author vividly recalls hearing Señor Lequerica of Spain describe this paragraph, in an Assembly debate, as 'the chastity belt of the Charter'. It has not proved a wholly effective device, and some of the bitterest UN debates have turned on the definition of 'intervention', 'domestic', and even 'essentially'. But it is there in black and white.

Crusaders for the 'federation of the world' that Tennyson

prophesied in 1842 in that otherwise somewhat racially chauvinist work, *Locksley Hall*, serve a wise as well as a noble cause. War will be finally outlawed only when the world accepts a supreme government. But some of these crusaders, less wise, have concentrated overmuch energy on the easy job of showing up the UN's faults. In part, this tendency has been a reaction against the idealizers' myth. One can understand the annoyance of a campaigner for world government when he comes up against people who think the UN already is one.

Even today some world-government enthusiasts argue that it is a mistake to try to develop the peace-keeping capacity of the UN as long as its basic constitutional structure remains unchanged. But as things stand, constitutional revision of the UN Charter is virtually impossible. Their attitude thus means relegating the whole effort to make the UN work more effectively to the deep-freeze, until the glorious day of the apocalyptic breakthrough.

It is odd that serious federalists should think this way. The historical pattern of development of existing federal systems points to the opposite conclusion. It is a pattern of small states at first forming a loose league, whose every member clung jealously to many attributes of sovereignty; of these leagues evolving, under various pressures, into closer unions; of strong central governments eventually emerging and encroaching bit by bit upon the members' prerogatives – not without resistance. Only in countries such as Canada and India, which had formerly been controlled by a single external power, have fully-fledged federal systems been launched at the outset of the country's independent career; and this is no model for the federation of the whole world, which – fortunately – has never been subjugated by one alien conqueror.

One might, then, expect the enthusiast for world federation to be a natural gradualist, not a perfectionist who spurns everything that is inadequate and embryonic and holds out for 'nothing but the best'. Impatience is understandable. But one does not speed the transformation of an acorn into an oak by putting it in a deep-freeze and waiting for a miracle.

Those who long for an effective world authority, but argue that the UN cannot grow into one and should therefore be given no encouragement to grow, are apt to find themselves in strange company: the company of political leaders who are anxious to curb the trend to greater activity in the UN by restoring the great powers' means of blocking this activity. These anxieties, as we have already noted and as will be shown in more detail, have been observable in London as well as in Moscow. On 5 February 1962 Macmillan told the House of Commons that

the United Nations can never be made to work unless political conditions can be created in the world which allow the Security Council to operate, not as a body permanently divided, but gradually as a team.

Despite the word 'gradually', that is a pretty fair statement of the perfectionist approach.

BRAVE OLD WORLD

One of the author's recurring experiences at UN headquarters in New York has been to hear diplomats sighing that it isn't at all like Geneva. These nostalgic veterans of the pre-war League of Nations are quite right: it isn't like Geneva. Nor, for that matter, was Geneva itself quite the cosy, gentlemanly club that they are really sighing for.

Naturally, the nostalgic veterans are Europeans. The United States never joined the League, and most of the Afro-Asian world was under European rule in the League's day. The atmosphere of the League, its centre of gravity, the bulk of the issues debated, and the two predominant members, Britain and France, were all European. How different from the UN of today, in its New York setting; its mounting membership of over a hundred states, half of them Asian and African; its two predominant members, America and Russia, although both deriving their character from a common European source, both defiant of much of the old European tradition.

Distance lends enchantment. The sighers for Geneva recall it not only as a scene of lost European predominance, but also as a quiet, well-mannered place; much more restful than the bright, brash UN with its raw new members, its tub-thumping and occasionally shoe-pounding Communists, its TV cameras and high-pitched commentators, and, not least, the infectious American zest for dragging discreet matters out into the open and dissecting them in public. The sighers tend to see cause and effect here, claiming that the League was quietly useful (or at least harmless) because it was European and that the UN is a dangerous runaway (or at best a failure) because the experienced, responsible, old-school Europeans are no longer in control.

This is a tempting way of working off the sense of frustration that loss of leadership involves. It is a dangerous temptation. To yield to it can lead to at least a half-conscious wish to see the UN run into trouble, or even collapse, in circumstances that would give the veterans the satisfaction of saying, 'We told you so' as the roof caves in on everybody, themselves included. And it is founded on yet another illusion – the traditional rose-tinted illusion about the good old days.

In the first place, the British at least were nothing like as fond of Geneva, when they had it, as some of them have become with the soft glow of fading memory. The late Lord (Robert) Cecil recorded, in *A Great Experiment*, that 'influential officials in the Foreign Office did not conceal their suspicion of the League'; and that his own colleagues in the Baldwin government

regarded it as a kind of excrescence which must be carefully prevented from having too much influence on our foreign policy. Geneva, to them, was a strange place in which a new-fangled machine existed in order to enable foreigners to influence or even control our international action. For us to do anything to help it either with money or diplomatic action was, in their view, an effort of national altruism which could rarely be justified. The League was officially tolerated. It was never liked.

The original British proposal was that the League Assembly should meet – briefly – only once every four years. Cecil notes that 'the great powers were obsessed with the wholly unreal danger that the small powers might band together and vote them down'.

Secondly, Geneva was often unquiet and at times ill-mannered. The League's early years were darkened by the raging conflicts in Eastern Europe that followed the Russian Revolution and the collapse of the Turkish Empire – conflicts in which France and Britain were extensively involved; by the Fascist seizure of power in Italy; by the bitter disputes over German reparations that brought French and Belgian troops into the Ruhr. Later came the general economic débâcle of the early 1930s, Japan's assault on China and Italy's on Ethiopia, the Spanish Civil War, the aggressive upsurge of Nazi Germany that forced the world into conflict.

Pre-war Europe was the source of most of the world's alarms, not its benevolent patron. And the League run by experienced and responsible Europeans proved no match for the encroaching forces of chaos, in Europe or elsewhere.

Today, there seems to linger, in many British and French minds in particular, a stubborn reluctance to face the fact that the world is no longer centred on Europe. America and Russia have now to be acknowledged as the two super-powers; but they can be accounted for as extensions of Europe. Industrial and military power is still, after all, concentrated in the 'greater Europe' thus defined; and what mastery of modern technology and political organization the under-developed countries have achieved can be, quite plausibly, attributed to European enterprise in spreading these things among them. An attitude commonly found in both Britain and France may be thus expressed: 'We recognize that the days of empire are over. We do not grudge the 'new nations' the paraphernalia of sovereignty. But we cannot seriously accept these poor, weak, jumped-up states as real members of the world community; and if the UN gives them the same voting power as our own great and ancient nations, we cannot take the UN seriously either'.

This attitude is to be distinguished from the 'good old rule' that Wordsworth rhymed – 'the simple plan, that those should take who have the power, that those should keep who can'; more simply still, that Might is Right. It is not a claim that the strong should actually rule the weak. Nor, on the other hand, is it a rejection of a claim that the weak should actually rule the strong; no such claim is being made.

What is asserted is that strong states will not bow to majority opinion on international questions in the way that individuals, however eminent, bow to majority opinion in a democratic country, even though the majority includes many ignorant and inexperienced people. In modern democracies, the privileged, the rich, the former wielders of private power, although they may still deploy great influence, have been brought to accept ultimate rule by majority. But, the argument runs, no such principle applies to the community of states, which lacks the shared interest and experience that bind a nation together, and which is too largely made up of states that cannot work democracy even at home.

One point about numbers should here be cleared away. UN Assembly voting is criticized for equating the large and the small (in terms of population) as well as the advanced and the backward. How absurd, it is said, that the 190 million Americans should thus be equated with say, the one and a half million Togolese. This complaint is often brought in to support the argument that the emergence of a mass of new Asian and African states has unbalanced the original UN structure. In fact this is a confusion of two quite distinct issues.

The 'new nations' include India, the world's second most populous country, and Indonesia and Pakistan, each with far more inhabitants than any West European country. The two UN members with the smallest populations of all are European: Iceland and Luxembourg. The founder members of 1945 included all the little Central American republics, whose combined population barely equals that of, say, Tanganyika.

Today Asia and Africa, which contain two thirds of the human race, still command only half the Assembly's votes. Latin-America, with only 7 per cent of the world's population, and Western Europe, with 10 per cent, have respectively 18 and 15 per cent of the votes. This representation is, however, more balanced than that of 1945, when Latin-America had two fifths of the votes, Asia and Africa less than a quarter. (Then as now, incidentally, Western Europe had a sixth, and the Soviet bloc a tenth.)

The equal voting power of midget states and giants alike has its effects *within* each group. Big Brazil is equated with tiny Panama, India with Laos, France with Luxembourg, Nigeria with Chad, Poland with Albania, Egypt with Lebanon. But it has little effect on the voting balance *between* groups. On the other hand, if the United States, by virtue of its great population, were given 120 Assembly votes to Togo's one, India would require 300 (while the total for Western Europe would be only 220), and China 460.

The real, but unstated, reason for the revival of complaints about 'unweighted' voting is that many new small members have taken a more independent line in their voting than did some of the original small members. (We shall discuss, later on, the revealing evidence that Russia has been just as aggrieved as the West by the independent attitude of these new nations, on whose support it had counted.)

But it is not really a 'numbers game' at all. At bottom, the complaint against the growing influence of the jumped-up new members in the UN rests on a doctrine much older than the Charter or the Covenant of the League. This is the traditional doctrine that peace-keeping is a job for great powers.

As a consciously expressed doctrine, this is in the straight line of descent from the Concert of Powers, comprising Britain, Habsburg Austria, Prussia, and Russia, that was devised after the Napoleonic wars to check any further irruptions into the re-established, legitimist world of early-nineteenth-century Europe. That concert was soon developed by Metternich of Austria and Tsar Alexander I into the rigidly authoritarian Holy Alliance, which proved too ultra-conservative for the stomachs of even the Tories of Britain 140 years ago. British and French sympathy and support were given to the successive revolts that eroded Metternich's system, brought into being such 'new nations' as Greece and Italy, and upset the vision of a world policed and disciplined by a group of backward-looking powers.

It is ironic to find echoes of Metternich's doctrine on the lips of British politicians today; and on the lips, too, of the leader of a Russia that has done away with its former tsars but not, it seems, with their dogmas.

The twisted course of Soviet policy towards the UN has had one constant feature: a jealous preoccupation with the privileges of great-power status. The powers' right of veto in the Security Council has been tirelessly described in Soviet statements as 'the cornerstone of the United Nations'. The 'special responsibility of the great powers for maintaining peace and security' is another official dogma still invariably asserted in Russia, where every sign of encroachment on the special position thus defined has been fiercely denounced.

Only recently has a matching British preoccupation emerged with similar frankness. In the UN's early years, British statesmen used to urge that use of the veto should be circumscribed. In November 1950 the Attlee government supported (admittedly without much enthusiasm) the Assembly's American-inspired 'Uniting for Peace' resolution, with its provision for emergency Assembly sessions if a Council decision on action to deal with a threat to peace was blocked by a veto. When this device – intended to prevent Soviet blocking of UN action in the event of any 'second Korea' – was first used, in 1956, after Britain and France had vetoed a Council resolution demanding a cease-fire in the Suez–Sinai conflict, British ministers made scathing comments about the Assembly; and at the Bermuda talks in the following spring they sought, unsuccessfully, American support for the restoration of the Council's primacy. But even in those strained times there was no clarion call such as Lord Home, then Foreign Secretary, sounded at Berwick in December 1961 for

a great new effort ... to bring the United Nations back to working the Charter as it was meant to be ... The founder members ... set up a Security Council to bear the primary responsibility for maintaining the peace. They named the great powers as permanent members in the expectation that they ... would deal together with any breach of the peace by the smaller powers.

This Metternichian tone was echoed by Harold Macmillan when he defended Lord Home in the Commons debate on 5 February 1962. He virtually repeated the passage here quoted from the Berwick speech, adding that 'the Security Council was to be, so to speak, the Cabinet of the world'.

There were two intriguing things about these two speeches. Where Home had in effect cried 'Back to the Council!' and 'Back to 1945!', Macmillan dwelt on the fact that

the effective operation of the Council has been made impossible by the Russian veto. ... The whole foundation on which the UN was built has been undermined. ... The Council has been made impotent, due to conditions having developed wholly contrary to what was thought likely in San Francisco in 1945. It is no good neglecting these facts. ...

Secondly, both ministers avoided any direct reference to the 'Uniting for Peace' device.

A muted resentment of this device emerged in the Prime Minister's complaint that 'the Assembly has tried to turn itself into something quite different from what was envisaged, namely, a kind of semi-executive authority. This has inherent dangers ...' Supporting him in the debate, an M.P. who had twice been a British delegate at the UN, Lady Tweedsmuir, said in explicit reference to the 'Uniting for Peace' resolution that 'This is where many troubles began'. But that was as far as it went.

A procedure accepted for over eleven years must, admittedly, be a difficult target at which to launch a frontal attack; the more difficult in view of Macmillan's recollection of the paralysis of the Council which the 'Uniting for Peace' procedure was designed to remedy; still more difficult, because this procedure had in fact proved unexpectedly effective, but in a way that the government would have found it embarrassing to acknowledge in public.

Only once since 1956* has the procedure been formally invoked to transfer a problem from Council to Assembly: that was in September 1960, when Khrushchev, literally at sea at the very start of his campaign against Hammarskjöld, ordered the vetoing of an Afro-Asian resolution that endorsed UN action in the Congo, and was promptly landed with an emergency Assembly whose every member (except France and South Africa) lined up solidly against the Soviet bloc.

The experiences of 1956, and of September 1960, sank home. The 'Uniting for Peace' procedure may have seemed to rust, almost unused; but, rusty or not, the weapon hangs over the heads of the veto-wielding Council members. Each of these, a latter-day Damocles, is now inclined, when on the point of vetoing a resolution that might bring it down upon him, to swivel a wary eye at the ceiling and think again.

Thus, Russia might well have vetoed the Council's Congo resolution of 21 February 1961 which strengthened the hand of a Secretary-General whom the Russians had just branded as a 'criminal', and Britain or France might well have vetoed the one of 24 November 1961, about which they expressed strong reservations, if in both these cases it had not been clear that an emergency Assembly would at once descend on their heads, so that a veto would merely force a vast number of governments to take a public stand against them. So Russia, France, and Britain abstained.

This explanation is necessary because without it British

* The 1958 emergency Assembly (on the Lebanon–Jordan crisis) was convened, by general agreement, without any explicit citing of the 'Uniting for Peace' resolution; this saved Russia's face (page 37).

policy in 1961–2 must seem incomprehensible. British ministers, particularly alarmed by UN action in the Congo, were demanding a 'return to the Council'; yet it was the Council, not the Assembly, that had mainly been shaping the Congo action. They were emphasizing the special status of the veto-wielding powers; yet, faced with proposals they intensely disliked, they failed to make use of that status. Britain had not cast a veto since Suez.

Macmillan's picture (page 29) of an impotent Council is likewise confusing, because it is outdated. The Council has been revived – by the Assembly. True, it is something of a zombie. The life that has been breathed into it is not its own. But the body that launched the Congo operation and passed five resolutions of increasing, indeed almost revolutionary, force on this question alone can hardly be described as 'paralysed by the Russian veto'. (Russia expressed serious doubts about two of these resolutions, while reluctantly voting for them, and abstained on two others.)

Here emerges the illusoriness, in the world of today, of the traditional idea of the great powers' special role in peace-keeping.

Undeniably, great powers do exist. They enjoy vast influence and vast military strength. How, then, does it come about that a major operation like the one the UN conducted in the Congo could be carried on, over a long period and through a whole series of different crises, *without* the unanimity between these powers which in Russian eyes is the UN's 'cornerstone'; *without* 'working the Charter as it was meant to be' – that is, in Lord Home's view, working through a united group of great powers that can 'deal together with' troublesome smaller fry?

The great-power powerlessness which makes nonsense of the traditionalist myth is partly explained by the nuclear deadlock; partly by the emergence of the host of new Asian and African states which, though still weak, represent a massive potential that is not to be casually alienated; and partly by a general restiveness among the 'middle powers' – not only among the formally 'non-aligned', but among many countries that now carry a certain weight in the world and are not minded to accept tamely the fiats of a select 'top' group.

The UN has not brought about these developments; but it reflects them. Both the Charter and the UN's subsequent record represent compromises between the great powers' claims to predominance, and the other states' resistance to these claims. The resistance has grown remarkably since 1945. When the Charter was signed the great powers were in effective military occupation of much of the earth's surface; the smaller states were mostly in confusion, war-torn or inert, newly renascent or still unborn. Since then the powers, while piling up their terrible weapons, have steadily lost ability to impose their will.

Gunboat diplomacy is not what it was. Witness the defiance of Russia first by Yugoslavia and then by still smaller Albania; the defiance of America by Cuba; Egypt's survival of quarrels with both Russia and America as well as of actual attack by Britain and France. There have even been signs of what Cecil had called the 'wholly unreal' prospect of small states banding together against all the great powers. In November 1961 seventy-one UN members carried an Assembly resolution urging the powers to refrain from further nuclear tests. Britain, France, Russia, and the United States all voted against it, but mustered only sixteen others to swell the opposition.

Clearly the UN cannot impose its will on the great powers where they stand on strong positions. But, equally, these powers, even when united, cannot expect always to impose their will on the UN. The mass of other members does not find them acceptable in the role of peace-keepers to all and sundry. Increasingly, as Hammarskjöld explained in 1960, the UN mechanism has been used to keep the great powers out of danger areas, not to get them in.

In this clear light, the vision of 'bringing the UN back' to the idea of the great powers 'dealing together with any breach of the peace by the smaller powers' fades into fantasy, a fantasy of the past. The UN Congo operation could not have been carried out through a Metternichian concert; the intervention of the powers was precisely what the operation was meant to avert. Not only the African states but the majority of other UN members too were anxious to secure this insulation.

There is very little that the backwardsmen can do now to bring the UN back to what it was 'meant to be'. The world has changed since 1945; and even in 1945 what you meant the UN to be depended on who you were. Today it is clear that, whatever the UN may in future become, it will not become the docile instrument of a cosy little club of Top Powers. The attempt to make the traditionalist myth a reality has come too late. The only effect of airing it is to annoy and alienate the great majority of the states of the world.

THE DOGMA IT WAS THAT DIED

The 'scientific' basis claimed for Marxism–Leninism has not saved Communist politicians from being misled by illusions about the UN. Some of the Soviet myths on the subject have been exploded already, some survive; but the awkward thing about them all is that, whenever the Moscow leadership adopts one, it necessarily acquires the status of a dogma – and the burying of a dead dogma is an unpleasant business.

Paradoxically, it was in the early 1950s, when the UN was most directly in conflict with Communist ambitions in Korea, that the organization was also most suspect in America as a supposed hotbed of Communism. To diehard isolationists, of course, it was always suspect. 'Anybody who speaks up for the United Nations,' once said the late Colonel McCormick of the *Chicago Tribune*, 'is either a Communist or misinformed.' But in 1952, with McCarthyism in full cry, a federal grand jury went so far as to allege that the UN had been infiltrated by 'an overwhelmingly large group of disloyal U.S. citizens'. (Out of 1,800 Americans in the Secretariat – most of them in low-grade, wholly non-political, posts – eighteen had refused to answer questions about their links, past or present, with Communist-run groups.) Threats of heavy-footed action by Congress eventually forced President Truman to order, and Secretary-General Trygve Lie to accept, an investigation of all Americans on the staff. No evidence was produced to support the charge that 'Communists in the UN' had somehow imperilled America's security; but some of the muck stuck.

Yet, throughout these years, Soviet spokesmen for their part were constantly complaining that the UN was dominated by 'aggressive imperialist forces' which prevailed in the Secretariat as well as in the Assembly.

When the Charter was being drafted, the Russians had been even less enthusiastic than the British about the Assembly. In 1950, the Soviet bloc was alone in voting against the 'Uniting for Peace' resolution. Moscow called it 'usurpation of the Council's prerogatives' and 'a crude violation of the Charter' which 'seriously imperilled peace'.

In those days, the Soviet line on the UN was simple and essentially defensive. In the Assembly, Russia could be outvoted; in the Council, thanks to the veto, it could not; therefore all power must be concentrated in the Council, however much this annoyed the smaller states. Any reform of the UN, whether by revision of the Charter or by such devices as Uniting for Peace, was liable to weaken Russia's defensive position; therefore there must be no changes made. The Charter was to remain immutable for all time, like the laws of the Medes and Persians.

If the UN, thus pickled, lapsed into disuse, the Russians would not grieve. With sour memories of the League, they regarded the UN essentially as an Anglo–American idea that had been pressed upon them, when they would have preferred a simple Metternichian concert of great powers. As long as the UN was there, they would naturally use its platform facilities (for which reason they then – ironically, as it turned out – strongly favoured having the headquarters in New York, rather than in Europe). But the thing must not be allowed to get out of hand.

Get out of hand it did, though the Russians, like others,

were slow to see the change coming. The UN action in Korea, although Moscow duly blasted it as 'criminally illegal', still fitted into the then accepted Soviet image of an organization which was regrettably western-dominated but included an impregnable special position for Russia. (It is still a speculative question how far the course of events in Korea was worked out in advance by a Soviet government that was well content to see America and China embroiled.) The 'Uniting for Peace' resolution, although bitterly opposed, was only a resolution; could a cumbrous talking-shop like the Assembly really make anything of it?

Then came 1956. The procedure Moscow had called 'usurpation' was suddenly used to conjure up an emergency Assembly on the Suez conflict. Russia gulped down its words and took part in this 'crude violation of the Charter'. By doing so, it virtually destroyed its own case against the calling of an emergency Assembly on Hungary, which followed almost at once.

Worse complications quickly arose. The Suez Assembly voted overwhelmingly in favour of the creation of the UN Emergency Force (UNEF). The idea of the Assembly thus encroaching on the Council's prerogatives in regard to the use of armed forces was anathema to Russia. In the circumstances, however, Russia could not stop it, and dared not even vote against it; for the plan was swept along on a human tide of smaller nations indignant against Britain and France, and impossible to dismiss as just another 'American-manipulated mechanical majority'. The 'special responsibility of the great powers' went by the board, and with it all the old insistence that it was for these powers to provide the UN with its sword-arm. UNEF, it was agreed at Hammarskjöld's suggestion, would be formed exclusively from the forces of the smaller states.

Moscow fumbled. Czechoslovak and Rumanian troops were offered, and discreetly declined by the Secretary-General. Slowly and awkwardly, Russia then withdrew to something like its original position on this question. Eventually it got round to denouncing UNEF as an 'illegal' creation, glossing over its own complicity. But it could not escape from its dilemma. In the summer of 1960, it was denouncing all idea of 'so-called UN forces' as an 'imperialist' machination against 'national liberation movements'. A few weeks after those words had been published in Moscow, Russia found itself voting (hesitantly) for the creation of the UN force for the Congo.

One dogma having died on its hands, the Soviet government found comfort in another. The wall of great-power privilege might have been breached; but was it not the manifest destiny of the 'new nations' who had helped in the breaching to align themselves with Russia, their natural champion, against the 'imperialist' West?

By 1958, it was noted in Moscow, the Afro-Asian states held a third of the Assembly's seats. This gave them 'a collective veto', since important Assembly resolutions require a majority of two to one, and can be defeated by 'a blocking third'. Soviet commentators gleefully argued that 'the American voting machine' was no longer working.

Thus the world saw, during the crisis over Lebanon and Jordan in the summer of 1958, the remarkable sight of Nikita Khrushchev actually proposing to transfer discussion of a threat to peace from the Council to an emergency Assembly.

This flouting of everything that Moscow had previously said about 'usurpation', 'violation', and 'illegality' occurred in complicated circumstances. Khrushchev at first, on 19 July, called for a 'summit' meeting, to be held in Geneva three days later, the participants to be America, Britain, France, India, Russia – and Hammarskjöld. (The Soviet leader emphasized that he did not wish to 'circumvent the UN'.) The American and British response was to suggest that heads of government should meet in the Security Council (which was already discussing Lebanon). Khrushchev agreed to this, provided Indian and Arab representatives took part. For a moment it looked as if he was really about to descend on New York.

A few hours before he accepted the Anglo–American proposal, however, the newspapers of Peking had denounced it as

> this deceptive plan ... full of pitfalls.... Most of the Council members are American-controlled, including the Kuomintang man who represents nobody except the moribund Chiang Kai-shek....

Two days later, without batting an eyelid, the Peking Press saved what face it could by standing on its head:

> The peace-loving peoples of the world welcome and support this proposal ... (and) hope that a special Security Council meeting with the participation of the heads of the five powers can be held as soon as possible.

But this was no more than face-saving. The Chinese Communists were in fact furious at the idea of thus upgrading the Council from which they were shut out. In America, meanwhile, Eisenhower and Dulles, who had no wish for a summit meeting either at this time or on this subject, were carefully cooling Khrushchev's ardour by insisting on 'Security Council rules'. He himself doubtless saw, as each day passed without the crisis worsening, either less chance of exploiting a summit or possibly less actual need for one. Firing off accusations of Western evasive tactics, he hastened to Peking on 31 July and spent three days making his peace there.

On 5 August he announced that he was demanding an emergency Assembly; one reason he gave for dropping the Council was that China's seat was occupied by 'a representative of a political corpse'. The relieved Americans were happy to cooperate in a move which came pretty close to use of the Uniting for Peace procedure, but was achieved without any embarrassing emphasis on Russia's belated conversion to the idea that some crises are better handled by the Assembly than by the Council.

In private, the Soviet delegates to this emergency Assembly were not at all pleased at its outcome. But they had to put a good face on it, because the Arabs had staged a grand mutual reconciliation in a state of apparent euphoria, and everybody else was expressing joy. (Even Hammarskjöld betrayed an unwonted exuberance.) Perhaps Gromyko's report to Khrushchev was more complacent than his private comments in New York. Anyway, the Soviet leader was evidently encouraged by this first experiment in upgrading the Assembly. Buoyed up by the belief that Afro-Asians who ventured to differ from America should be ready for a lead from Russia, he decided to start taking the Assembly seriously.

In both 1959 and 1960 he turned the force of his own personality on to it. In 1959 he made only a brief appearance, but it was not the mere formal visit to the Assembly that most heads of state or government make when they happen to be in America during its sessions. He used his one speech to launch the new Soviet proposal for general disarmament. The launching was impressive; but the seven weeks of debate on disarmament that followed left most questions about the new plan still unanswered, and the whole fine-sounding but fuzzy proposal was passed on to the ten-power talks at Geneva that had been arranged before Khrushchev's Assembly speech. It seemed that to Russia the Assembly was essentially still only a sounding-board. But by the time Khrushchev returned to New York a year later, much in Soviet UN policy had changed.

Up to mid 1960 it was still Soviet dogma that the Charter was sacred. A book on the UN by Grigory Morozov* published in Moscow that summer repeated the ritual formula: 'The Charter contains all that is needed for the UN to provide effective guarantees of peace and security.' Morozov devoted much of his book to denouncing every kind of proposal for Charter revision, and portrayed Russia as the defender of the faith of San Francisco against those who 'seek to revise it ... because the Charter is a serious obstacle to their aggressive plans'.

The same Morozov, not long afterwards, was declaring

* *Organizatsia Obyedinyennikh Natsiy*, Institute of International Relations, Moscow, 1960. Introduction by Academician A. V. Topchiev.

on Moscow radio that 'the structure of the UN and the articles of its Charter must be changed'.

On the face of it, this abrupt reversal of policy arose from the course of UN action in the Congo, with particular reference to the Katanga, during August 1960. In August the Moscow Press launched an angry campaign of personal charges against Hammarskjöld. In mid September Valerian Zorin, Soviet deputy foreign minister, devoted two speeches at the UN to branding him as a 'servant of the colonialists'. On 23 September Khrushchev told the Assembly that 'the post of Secretary-General ... should be abolished', and that there should be created, instead, 'a collective executive body of the UN comprising three persons, each of whom would represent a certain group of states'.

This 'troika' plan involved, of course, a drastic bit of Charter revision. The Charter not only specifies that there shall be a single Secretary-General; it also lays down that no Secretariat official shall take instructions from any government, and that no government shall seek to influence individual officials.

Khrushchev expressed concern about more than the Congo. Russia, he said, now accepted the Western and neutralist thesis that disarmament must be accompanied by 'the creation of armed forces under international control to be used by the UN'. These forces might be 'used for reactionary purposes' unless the UN executive was reshaped as a 'troika'.

Poor Morozov. The ink was only a few weeks dry on a passage in his book which complained indignantly that 'to speak as if some kind of defect in the Charter would hinder disarmament means, to say the least, to display elementary bad faith'.

The events in the Congo had in fact brought to a head a more general Soviet disenchantment about the UN. The 'new nations', and particularly the non-aligned ones, had certainly gained strength; but they were not using their strength, as the dogma said they should, to back up Russia's lead. On the contrary, just as Khrushchev was landing in

New York on 19 September, Zorin had thrown in the Soviet towel and withdrawn a resolution he had presented to an emergency Assembly session on the Congo accusing Hammarskjöld of failing to carry out his mandate. At one o'clock the next morning, the Assembly carried over Zorin's protests a resolution that asked the Secretary-General to 'continue to take vigorous action'. This resolution was moved by Alex Quaison-Sackey of Ghana, and co-sponsored by seventeen Asian and African states; and every one of the Afro-Asians was among the seventy states that voted for it.

During the three weeks that Khrushchev spent at the 1960 Assembly he repeatedly returned to the charge against Hammarskjöld. But neither then, nor even in the spring of 1961 when the murder of Patrice Lumumba had evoked bitter anger among many Africans and others, did Russia dare to demand an Assembly vote on its charges against Hammarskjöld or its 'troika' plan for the Secretariat. One after another, the non-aligned Asian and African countries took a public stand against the Soviet plan. On 15 April 1961, in an Assembly debate on an Afro-Asian resolution on the Congo, Guinea, backed by Russia, insisted on challenging a paragraph which specifically assigned executive action to Hammarskjöld (who by then was being completely boy-cotted by the Russians). By eighty-three votes to eleven (the nine Soviet bloc votes, Cuba, and Guinea) the Assembly overrode the challenge, the vast majority of the Asians and Africans once again lining up solidly against Russia.

It would be rash to assume that we have heard the last of the troika. When, after Hammarskjöld's violent death in September 1961, the pressing problems of the Congo made it a matter of great urgency to appoint a successor, the Russians naturally tried to exploit the situation to force the adoption of their plan. But even in those harsh circum-stances they could make no real progress; after six weeks of haggling, they reluctantly accepted U Thant as acting Secretary-General to serve for the remaining year and a half of the five-year term of office.

Their attempts – which failed – to tie Thant's hands by

making it impossible for him to act without the consent of his Soviet assistant, and their insistence on a short term, finally disposed of all idea that their troika plan really sprang from a belief that Hammarskjöld was a 'tool of the imperialists'. His successor, a man from a non-aligned Asian country, with an impeccable background in Burma's own struggle for independence, was still, in their eyes, unreliable. The long haggle over his instalment in office was a public sign of the death of the second Soviet dogma – the illusory belief that the growing influence of the new Asian and African members made the UN ripe for a take-over bid.

As we have seen, that illusion had already begun to fade in 1960. When Khrushchev first put forward the 'troika' plan, he made much of the argument that it was in the interests of the non-aligned Asian and African states as well as of the Communist ones. They were not convinced. From the non-aligned states' point of view, the UN was already evolving in the right direction. Their voting power in the Assembly was growing steadily as new members came in. The Congo operation was essentially theirs; they supplied the troops, their nationals filled most of the key military and civilian posts, they sat on Hammarskjöld's advisory committee, they drafted and moved the Council resolutions. They welcomed the general enlargement of the role of both small nations and Secretariat. Most of them trusted Hammarskjöld even when they did not see eye to eye with him. And now, with these satisfactory changes proceeding, they found Russia demanding new great-power shackles for the Secretariat.

The question naturally presented itself: why now? When the West was visibly strong in the UN, the Russians had neither denounced Hammarskjöld as its accomplice, nor tried to shackle the Secretariat. Yet, with the decline of the West, Khrushchev was sounding the alarm. Was it that the Russians were more worried by UN decisions mainly shaped by the non-aligned than they had been by decisions taken in the days of western predominance? On reflection, this seemed a very real possibility. Russia had been able to count on a good deal of sympathy in uncommitted Asia and Africa when it flatly rejected Western-shaped UN decisions; but it could hardly keep that sympathy if it was going to resist, regularly and publicly, decisions mainly shaped by the 'new nations' themselves. It was logical enough for Khrushchev to seek a 'hidden veto' inside the Secretariat, where there would be no public spectacle of Soviet blocking tactics, but merely silent obstruction behind the scenes.

Disenchantment has in fact carried Moscow's backwardsmen even further into the Metternichian past than their Western counterparts. It is not enough, in Khrushchev's eyes, to get back to 'working the Charter as it was meant to be'. The great-power position, menaced by the emergence of vigorous small-nation support for an executive that is not the kind the powers intended to create, must be reinforced by extending the veto into the Secretariat as well as clinging to it in the Council.*

Although prophecy is always rash, it seems that yet another disenchantment awaits Moscow. The present mood of the mass of smaller nations suggests that there is even less chance of revising the Charter in order to buttress great-power privilege than of getting back to a restrictive interpretation of it for the same purpose. The 'troika' may yet be trotted out again; but it is not likely that we shall ever see this creaking equipage win the UN race.

* In 1963 Russia showed great anxiety to assert the Council's authority over the UN observation mission in Yemen, although Thant had already reached agreement with the Arab governments involved in the Yemen conflict, and the first elements of the UN mission – manned mainly by Yugoslavs and Canadians – had actually been organized before the Council debated the matter.

3 · *Mice and a White Horse*

So much for myth. Let us start in on truth; noting, first, that the great-power conflicts have not prevented the growth of a limited but important UN power of executive action – a process in which smaller nations have played unexpectedly vigorous parts. How has this happened, and how far has it gone?

New York taxi drivers are strongly individual types, but they seem to have at least one habit in common. The driver who is taking you to the UN building is apt to break off his own monologue when there is only a block or two to go, and ask in a tone that clearly expects a straight answer: 'What *are* they doing in there, can *you* tell me?'

In the UN's first years – before it set up headquarters in the midtown Manhattan area between the East River and First Avenue known as Turtle Bay – such a question could be answered pretty simply, though not very encouragingly. In 1948, when the Assembly met in Paris, the French newspaper *Combat* sketched the essentials of 'l'ONU' thus:

> Onuland is a mountainous little country lying on the eastern frontier of the Trocadero. It is an industrialized country. It produces mimeographed copies of speeches, and hopes in the near future to produce an extremely rare substance called peace. ...

This pithy description is no longer adequate. Certainly Onuland is still a major producer of words, both spoken and on paper. But the *Onusiens* (as they have become known in the Congo) have burst out of their densely peopled little territory; and their diaspora, now scattered across the world, has turned its hand to many new trades. Although the population of Turtle Bay itself has grown, it is now greatly outnumbered by the thousands serving the UN in various capacities 'in the field' from Chile to Korea. The thunder of oratory (and mimeograph machines) from headquarters is faint in the ears of these distant *Onusiens*, whose tasks involve more perspiration than peroration; and if the ink of copious reporting and documentation often mingles with their sweat, so too, in some cases, does a not negligible stream of their blood.

This book is concerned with the political side of the UN and will therefore refer only briefly to the large group among the 'men in the field' working on technical assistance and other economic and social tasks, mainly in the under-developed countries.* But it must be noted that the UN's political and non-political forms of fieldwork often overlap and interplay. Sometimes this is obvious, as in the case of its efforts to make peace between Israel and the Arab states and its relief of nearly a million Palestine refugees; sometimes less obvious, as in the case of Laos (page 115); sometimes simply implicit, as in the plain fact that any easing of economic and social strains in weak little states is likely to reduce the risk of a political conflict or collapse that might lead to international trouble.

Dag Hammarskjöld, when asked to define a 'UN presence', held firmly to what he called the 'completely pragmatic' view that 'there is a UN presence whenever the UN is present'. It is hard to think of any more precise formula that would cover all its recent variations. They range from such modest 'outposts' as the Secretary-General's representatives in Jordan, East and Central Africa, and Laos, by way of the observer group in Kashmir and the truce-supervision staff based in Jerusalem, to the international force on the Gaza-Aqaba line and the massive Congo operation; this last has comprised large-scale economic activities as well as ground and air forces which at one point in 1962 were around 20,000 strong.

This diaspora has been an unforeseen growth. The executive arm that the UN has acquired in the peace-keeping field is not the one that was envisaged when the

* Altogether, 16,500 out of the 18,000 people employed by the UN and its agencies do non-political work.

Charter was drawn up in 1945. Yet the Charter has not been changed by so much as a comma, and the prospects of its being changed are remote. It is the world that has changed, and, in so doing, has swept away virtually every trace of the peace-keeping arm planned in 1945 – except for a nameplate on the thirty-fifth floor of the UN building.

The Charter laid down that, if a threat to peace and security could not be removed by peaceful means, the UN could use armed forces that would be directed by a Military Staff Committee representing the five permanent Council members – America, Britain, China, France, and Russia. Not only would the Big Five, through their veto power in the Council, make sure that no UN force could be used against either themselves or their favoured friends; they were also to have direct joint control of any such force. And their intention, as they stated it at the San Francisco conference, was that not even preliminary peace-keeping action – not even the investigation of a complaint – should be possible without their unanimous approval.*

In vain did a Mexican at San Francisco point out that all this meant 'a world order in which the mice could be stamped out but the lions would not be restrained'. The mice had to take it or leave it. The lions, then very much in their pride, said that they were going to do the lion's share of the job of peace-keeping and therefore had a right to hog the control of it.

But the best-laid schemes of lions, too, gang aft a-gley, and this was not one of the best-laid. The Military Staff Committee was defeated – by the task of agreeing on the

* Four of the Five would probably have yielded to the smaller nations' pleas that investigation, at least, should be veto-free; but Russia was adamant. Andrey Gromyko, indeed, had the other Four thoroughly alarmed for several days by insisting that even discussion of a case must be subject to veto. Secretary of State Stettinius called this a 'very serious crisis' and said the Soviet demand 'would make a farce' of the whole UN. Eventually Harry Hopkins and Averell Harriman took it up in Moscow with Stalin in person. Stalin said it was 'insignificant'. Next day Gromyko dropped the demand.

size and shape of the armed forces it was to direct. The Americans stood out (by themselves) for large forces; which was unrealistic and needless, as the veto was going to prevent these UN forces being used against any state that could get one of the Big Five to shield it (and there were few that could not). The Russians were obstructive about everything else. By 1947 the generals and admirals who formed the Committee were in complete deadlock; in 1948, with military bluntness, they admitted it.

Solemnly, every year since then, the Big Five have appointed to the Committee a glittering array of top brass – U.S. Air Force generals, Soviet colonel-generals, Chinese lieutenant-generals, French *contre-amiraux*, British air vice-marshals. Officially, these stars sing together fortnightly throughout the year. In practice, behind the nameplate there is a deep silence.

True, the drafters of the Charter, perhaps foreseeing some delay in this matter – though not, one imagines, a delay of two decades – provided that, if need arose before the UN was duly supplied with the armed forces envisaged in Article 43, the Big Five would maintain peace by joint action on behalf of the UN, under Article 106. But this 'transitional security arrangement' has become as much of a dead letter as the main Charter provision for enforcement.

We have now looked at two of the more disquieting truths about the 'League with teeth' that was shaped in 1945. First, it has never been fitted with the dentures that were designed for it. Secondly, if it had been, it would still be limited to taking only small bites.

With even its few Charter teeth missing, the UN might naturally be thought doomed to remain a 'mere debating society', a mumbling talk-shop, its Council 'paralysed by the veto', its Assembly powerless to do more than – as a British minister pointed out with noble scorn in 1956 – 'make recommendations'. Mere moral authority, as we have seen, has limitations that are all the more severe when, as is visibly the case, the world sees no particular moral superiority in the assemblage of busy horse-traders at Turtle

Bay. Even if the inhabitants of that strange glass-walled
enclave in Manhattan to some extent made good a claim
that it was a kind of Vatican City built into a latter-day
Rome, they would face the equivalent of Stalin's reputed
gibe: 'How many divisions has the Pope?'

It is here that – life prevailing over logic – the UN begins
to spring its surprises. The Military Staff Committee's brilliant array of general officers may be a mere notion behind
a time-worn nameplate. The Korean campaign, a fading
memory after a decade of swift change, may be dismissed as
a confusing exception to all the rules, unique and unrepeat-
able. But who then are all these generals who have served
under the UN flag during the past few years – serving not by
ghostly attendance at notional meetings, but by practical,
professional command and staff duty, often in arduous and
sometimes in dangerous circumstances? Who, then, are
Generals Burns, Bennike, Martola, Bull, von Horn, Gyani,
Nimmo, Iyassu, Gebre, Prem Chand, Kettani, Alexander,
McKeown?

There have been, admittedly, few divisions behind these
generals. But it is, perhaps, more significant that there have
been few divisions between them. The top brass on the
Military Staff Committee represents a group of powers
which, together, command overwhelming military might
but which are still, after all these years, deadlocked on the
question of how to place any of it at the service of the UN.
The UN's 'working generals', on the other hand, have
virtually all been provided by smaller nations, such as
Australia, Canada, Denmark, Ethiopia, Finland, India,
Ireland, Morocco, Norway, Pakistan, Sweden. Their
soldiers and observer corps and airmen have been of still
more varied national origins. What links them is a general
agreement that there is a job to be done in the name of the
UN and a general will to get on with it.

The mice, in fact, tired of waiting respectfully for the
lions, have begun to move in.

The beginning of the process may be seen in Palestine in
1948–9, when the great powers signally failed to honour the

Council's 'primary responsibility' for maintaining peace in an area for which the UN had become particularly responsible. Although America and Russia had both pushed the partition plan through the Assembly, they did little or nothing to strengthen the UN's hand when its authority was violently defied. Count Folke Bernadotte of Sweden, who as UN Mediator went literally into the firing-line, was assassinated by terrorists. Ralph Bunche of the UN Secretariat then carried the task of mediation through to the conclusion of a set of armistices in 1949 between Israel and the Arab states. Bernadotte's tragic death and Bunche's Nobel Peace Prize were symbols of the emerging pattern – a pattern of active fieldwork for peace by men drawn from small nations, not closely identified with any great power, and from the Secretariat.

Korea was not entirely irrelevant to this trend. Although a predominantly American operation, it drew many small nations into active roles in an international framework. And it precipitated the 'Uniting for Peace' resolution, which Secretary-General Trygve Lie later called 'a profoundly important shift of emergency power from the veto-ridden Security Council to the veto-less General Assembly – a shift the full potentialities of which have still to be realized'.

When Andrey Vishinsky was vainly leading the Soviet opposition to the 'Uniting for Peace' proposal, he waxed particularly bitter about one of its provisions which most people at the time thought pretty innocuous (and which, indeed, had no visible effect). It asked Trygve Lie to form a panel of military experts from whom governments could get advice about maintaining units of their forces in readiness for UN service. Vishinsky denounced it as

fundamentally incompatible with the Charter. It short-circuits the Military Staff Committee and the Security Council ... The military experts will be at the beck and call of the Secretary-General. He is to be Commander-in-Chief of the armed forces of the Assembly ... riding on a white horse. ... Under the Charter, he can command only his Secretarial staff.... One does not need military experts to run mimeograph machines.

Prophetic words. Vishinsky died – suddenly, at the UN – in 1955. He did not live to see Hammarskjöld conjuring up an international UN force for Sinai in 1956, and a larger one for the Congo in 1960, setting up map-lined operations rooms on the thirty-eighth floor of the UN building, recruiting a cosmopolitan staff to direct far-flung military movements, personally spearheading the UN troops' entry into a hostile Katanga (riding a white, winged work-horse in the form of a Convair) – and dying on the Congo border in 1961, in circumstances which in a national context would be classed as 'on active service'.

The mice and the mimeographers had by then got over 20,000 men under arms in UN service. The great powers who were to have provided the UN's sword-arm were specifically barred from contributing troops to these forces. Three of these powers – Britain, France, and Russia – were, at best, ambivalent in their attitudes to the UN forces and their tasks. UNEF, the force that had steadied the Egypt–Israel border for five years, had been authorized by the Assembly, by a procedure that Russia denounced as illegal, after British and French vetoes had stymied the Council. The Congo force had been authorized by the Council – but by a Council painfully aware that a veto would bring the Assembly into play (Britain and France had abstained in the authorizing vote, and Russia had visibly hesitated; later, Russia vainly demanded the complete removal of the force from the Congo). The direction of the UN forces was in the hands not of the great powers but of the Secretary-General, advised by committees that represented only smaller nations and which he had appointed himself.*

These international armed forces are the most eye-catching but not the only part of the UN's unforeseen executive arm. The same pattern of partnership between

---

* In 1962 agreements were negotiated between the Secretary-General, Indonesia, and the Netherlands for the sending of another UN force to West New Guinea (Irian) and for a temporary UN administration there. These agreements, subsequently referred to the Assembly for ratification, created a further precedent for executive action.

Secretariat and smaller nations is to be seen in the observer group that operated for six months in 1958 in Lebanon, in the truce-supervision teams on Israel's borders, and in the civilian side of the Congo operation. There are other, even less conspicuous, instances. The least conspicuous, naturally, are those that do not involve any sending of a UN 'presence' into the field at all, those in which the trick is worked entirely at headquarters, and often behind the scenes.

It is easy to see, and say, how limited the UN executive capacity still is; how much it depends on improvisation from slender resources, on appeals to states and statesmen for help which they are not obliged to give, and, above all, on a few not infallible individuals. The Secretary-General and whoever else, on his staff or outside it, may play a controversial key-role in a UN operation that angers a member government, are in highly vulnerable positions. Almost any action, or indeed inaction, is bound to annoy some party, for the merest breath of UN intervention is liable to influence matters one way or the other.

What is less easy to see and explain is how UN action on such a basis is possible at all, and how far it can go. Generally speaking, it requires a fairly broad consensus among the member governments as well as a generous but not imprudent interpretation of the Charter and of existing precedents. The consensus may be no more than tacit. Some governments may express strong reservations, while not going so far as to oppose the executive move flatly. The Secretariat and its associates then have to make a nice calculation: to what extent are these reservations being made merely for effect, or for the record; to what extent do they reveal that the intended move is going to run into entrenched opposition?

Thus we come back to the 'talk-shop' on Turtle Bay. It would be absurd to call this babbling building the UN's power-house; such modest power as there is behind the UN's elbow comes from the real world outside its glassy walls. But the gathering in the Assembly, and the presence in New York of the members' permanent missions when the

Assembly is not sitting, provide a clearing-house. When an executive move is contemplated, the question whether there is enough of a consensus to support it can be explored at several different levels: formally, in public debate; less publicly, in systematic private consultation with all parties; or, one might say, intuitively, by simply judging what will be the general reaction to a move about which it may be better not to hold explicit consultations in advance. This calls for knowledge of the real workings of the talk-shop, and of the balance of forces within it.

4 · The Monster of Turtle Bay

WORDS, NOT DEEDS

IN the first place, the talk-shop talks. A great weariness afflicts the soul at the sheer volume of verbiage from an Assembly in full spate, with all its main committees going at it simultaneously in the row of basement rooms. The word 'committee', suggestive of a compact group getting down to business round a table, is misleading. The seven main committees, in which the bulk of an Assembly's debating is done, are all committees of the whole. Each, therefore, has over a hundred members (not to mention their advisers), disposed in semi-circular rows throughout a vast room. Members speak from their seats instead of marching down the aisle to stand at a rostrum, as is done in plenary sessions; but this saves nothing except marching time. Seated, a 'speaker' will drone just as soporifically through the reading of a long prepared speech. He is immune even from tiredness in the legs.

Whether anybody is actually listening to an average speech is hard to tell. Long ago, the newspapers got a few candid photographs of delegates visibly slumbering in their seats, and since then most delegates have learnt how to pass into coma with open, if slightly glazed eyes; others use dark glasses. Those who are observably awake are often reading, writing, or quietly conferring with colleagues. You have to get pretty close to tell whether this activity is concerned with urgent diplomatic business or with plans for their next vacation. And I have, on occasion, seen a 'speaker' so bored with the text he had to read out that he was himself doodling while reading it.

A UN debate can be gruellingly repetitive. It is bad enough to hear the same man make the same speech on the same subject year after year. Worse, in the course of one Assembly he may say it all half a dozen times: first in the opening 'general debate'; second in discussing whether his pet item is to be debated; then in an opening statement in committee; then again in committee, after a resolution has been proposed; again in explanation of his vote; and once or twice more when the resolution comes before a plenary session.

Attempts have been made to cut down this vain repetition. Mongi Slim of Tunisia, who presided over the marathon 155-day Assembly of 1961–2, survived to urge upon his fellow delegates some time-saving procedures the fate of which is uncertain at the time of writing. But there is no hope of any such drastic change as was once suggested in a light-hearted article in the journal of the British UN Association by George Steiner, which began:

The ancient Parthians poured molten gold down the throats of those of their country who spoke longer than was deemed fit in public council. And in seventeenth-century New England, loquacity was often punished in the ducking-stool. If these practices were yet in force, the corridors of the United Nations would be filled with precious cadavers or men shaking water out of their ears.*

Steiner simply proposed making UN speakers buy their time, the fees paid to go into the technical assistance funds: 'Soon the hot air of rhetoric might be turning wheels in under-developed Zanzibar.' Enchanted with the idea, *The Economist* worked it up a bit more, recommending, in fairness to the poorer nations, a few minutes free of charge for each orator ('what is worth saying can be said in a few minutes'), a steeply rising scale of charges for additional eloquence, and a device to cut off all microphones and interpretation circuits 'the instant an orator's cash payment, previously inserted into a coin-box, ran out'. Finance ministers, it was argued, would soon learn to discipline their delegates; and 'short, pithy Assemblies might recapture the public attention and respect that long-winded ones have lost'.

* *United Nations News*, October 1955.

Note that these pleas for brevity were made when the Assembly was still only sixty strong. It would be wrong to suppose that the founder members were a crisp, taciturn lot, and the logorrhea has set in only with the entry of a mass of newcomers. The longest winded are in fact mostly found among the longest seated.

The Russians, who think nothing when on their home ground of listening to Khrushchev throughout two solid days of a congress, probably stand amazed at their own restraint in UN speechmaking. But non-Soviet man, not being adjusted to the Russian habit of dealing out time, like other things, in large lumps, and not having had the invaluable training of waiting for food in Moscow restaurants, still winces at the Soviet performance; especially as it comes in triplicate (U.S.S.R., Ukraine, Byelorussia),* with further identical copies provided by the delegations of other Soviet-bloc countries. Many Soviet behaviour patterns at the UN have changed since the historic day, in 1954, when Vishinsky accepted a drink at the delegates' bar for the first time. Russian delegates, who once used to charge set-faced through the lobbies in flying wedges, have learnt to relax – up to a point. But heavy oratory, like slow-motion meal service, is a Russian tradition that existed long before the Soviet system and may well outlast it.

What hurts is the need to listen carefully through the repetitious jargon of Soviet speeches, just in case some shift in the party line is to be detected. (One can seldom get far by just buttonholing a Russian delegate and asking if a speech was *meant* to make a new point). It is less of an ordeal to suffer the formidable eloquence of some of the Latin-Americans. Those among them who revel in the elaboration of lofty sentiments are generally the least

* Stalin originally demanded that each of the Soviet Union's sixteen republics should have a UN seat and vote. The three that he eventually got are a strange anomaly. The UN has even been honoured with visits by the 'Foreign Ministers' of the Ukraine and Byelorussia; it has never been discovered how these statesmen occupy themselves in between trips to New York.

likely to say anything that makes the Assembly sit up and take notice.

It is of one of the veteran Latin-American delegates that a classic UN story is told: how another delegate accidentally picked up the text of the speech the Latin-American had just made, and found it marginally annotated almost like a musical score, with one passage heavily marked: 'Weak point. Shout'. Around Dr Victor Belaunde of Peru, whose bravura performances are in a class by themselves, a whole body of legend has grown up. He presided over the 1959 Assembly, which completed its business by 13 December, achieving a brevity unmatched in recent years; and there were some who said unkindly that this was mainly due to Belaunde's elevation to the podium, where he had to hold himself in. (It may also have been that he made a good president. Some of the more turgid orators are, at the same time, experienced and valuable diplomats whose efforts behind the scenes often save the Assembly from wasting time in blind alleys.)

Long before the great increase in membership began, one of the toiling simultaneous interpreters – who often achieve an actual improvement of the delegates' prose – let his tongue slip in a way that created another classic, as well as suggesting a cry from the heart. The debate was on disarmament; and one of the speakers was rendered as having appealed for 'the regulation, limitation, reduction, and ultimate abolition of arguments'.

By 1957 it seemed that this cry from the heart was beginning to be heard. The number of member states, having risen only from fifty-one to sixty between 1945 and 1955, then shot up to eighty-two by 1957. The new members may not have been much less wordy than the old ones, but the pressure on time certainly became more obvious. The 1957 Assembly uprooted some of the recurring 'hardy perennials' on the agenda and agreed to leave them alone for a year or two, or if possible even longer. It was particularly keen to get free of the debates on abstract principles and definitions that had led previous

Assemblies into scholastic disputation; for example, about the precise definition of 'aggression' – which remains undefined to this day.

The tide of talk still rolls on. One delegate, a man hardened by years of diplomacy, moved me to pity half-way through an Assembly session by saying that sometimes, as the wordy waves beat upon his head, he felt he was dying, 'especially in the afternoons'. In most national parliaments members simply stay away from dull debates in which they have no special interest. The UN delegates are less free, because they are representatives of governments. However dull the debate, they cannot afford to miss too much of it; for one thing, they will have to report on it.

The main reason for dullness is, of course, this fact that they are representatives. Any important speech has to be officially approved to ensure that it is an accurate reflection of government policy. Even as sophisticated and witty a speaker as Adlai Stevenson has to bear this cross; it seems a refined cruelty to lay it on anyone who really knows how to make a speech a work of art. Few delegates – Krishna Menon springs to mind – feel so little need to bother about their own governments' sensibilities that they can extemporize freely. (In Menon's case the results have not always been happy; but even some of his critics concede that at several sessions he has provided the only antidote to boredom.)

Speeches are also dull because the speaker is talking to several quite different audiences: to his fellow delegates, among whom he is seeking support for whatever he is up to; to public opinion at home, which needs to be reassured that its government, while moved by the highest ideals, is not for one moment going to relax its pursuit of national interests; and to the public in other countries, which he would like to impress with the fact that his government is ever ready to negotiate, but quite unyielding in its convictions. (He does not really need to bother much with this last audience. As a rule, the Press of each country reports a certain number of its own delegates' speeches, a few of those made by Americans and Russians, and nobody else's – unless they are exceptionally favourable or, if hostile, exceptionally silly and good for gibes.)

There are, of course, the big moments. But when the great men do descend on the UN, they are liable to crowd each other out. The clearest proof of this was provided when in September 1960 Khrushchev's example brought a flock of heads of government to the Assembly. Two dozen of them made speeches which, taken together, did nothing to raise the level of debate, and some of which went virtually unreported.

One could not use the word 'dull' about a session that began with Fidel Castro and his bodyguard storming into the UN building, the night before opening day, and threatening to bed down in the lounge if their hotel problems were not immediately solved; and during which Khrushchev heckled Macmillan, took off a shoe to pound his desk with, and stormed away at Hammarskjöld, demanding not merely his resignation but the abolition of his office. But the effect of the antics and threats was not to focus world attention on the real issues, but to distract it, and to make serious debate almost impossible until the circus had left town.

While the 'greatest show on earth' lasted, it was largely a publicity contest between the members of an all-star cast; and even personalities such as, say, Gomulka of Poland, who would have caught every eye if he could have come to the UN on his own, were lost to view. A poignant memory of the second day of that Assembly lingers: the sight of Marshal Tito sitting, unremarked, in a corner of the Press bar, and having to wait a clear five minutes before he was spotted by photographers (one assumes he had gone there to be spotted; he looked very happy when he was). Even more poignant was the fate of Menon, then the recognized Hamlet in the regular stock company. Normally a swirl of interest attended his first appearance of the season, but this time, happening to arrive just when Castro and his bearded, battle-dressed troupe had invaded the building, he found himself alone and ignored.

But normally there are no stars (in the sense of dominant personalities) and few character actors in the Turtle Bay show. The Assembly is a parliament of diplomats;* and in such a parliament there is little room for the eccentrics and colourful personalities who spice many national legislatures. In fact, delegates tend to a remarkable sameness. The article in *Combat* already quoted (page 43) remarked that

all the Onulanders resemble one another; they all have the same physical appearance, the same clothes, and mostly the same spectacles.... From which one can see that Onulande is a very old country, and that its people have achieved an unparalleled ethnic unity.

One Assembly president told me that it was a recurring anxiety that, at the end of a long and soporific speech, the president would forget who had made it and call the same delegate to speak again. From the presidential seat on the high podium, above and behind the delegate who is addressing a plenary session, most speakers tended to look much the same – the same pair of shoulders in a well-cut dark suit, and above them, all too often, virtually the same bald patch.

By convention, all delegates are distinguished; as a British M.P. in debate refers to a colleague as 'the honourable Member', so in UN debate one refers to 'the distinguished delegate'. It does not necessarily follow that all delegates are easily distinguished, any more than all M.P.s are easily honoured. Moreover, as a good part of their verbiage is made up of unexceptionable platitudes, one can sometimes enter a committee room in the middle of a speech and listen to it, or to an interpretation of it, through headphones for several minutes without any idea which of the hundred seated delegates is making it.

Colourless flatness has its perils; bored delegates may

* Dean Rusk, later American Secretary of State, was (in 1955) the first to use the expression 'parliamentary diplomacy' to describe its operations.

become bad-tempered and a bored public indifferent. Rows make news; and they can have a stimulating effect on delegates as well as on the general public outside. 'Everybody likes a fight, especially about peace.'* There is an important exception to this rule: when the same verbal fight comes round too often, in the same terms, and without any noticeable effect on actual events. But, boring as repetitious rows may be, and much though the Assembly has been criticized for returning again and again to debate the wrongs done to Hungary, to non-whites in South Africa, to Tibet, and so on, it is hard to prove even in cases like these that its debates will have no effect at all in the long run. Other cases are on record – such as Cyprus and Algeria – where, after the Assembly had persisted in staging yearly debates despite many warnings of their futility, change did eventually come; and those who favoured change remain unconvinced that it would have come more easily if silence had reigned at the UN.

Whether making news through rows, or vanishing behind clouds of tedium, whether sharply divided or for a moment united, the Turtle Bay talk-shop is still a mirror of the world in which we have to live. It is not a perfect mirror, but it is the best we have; for some purposes the only one we have. Its flaws are obvious; but, often, when its proceedings cause annoyance or anger, it is not because of the flaws, but because it is mirroring the real world too truthfully. People like to persuade themselves not only that they are right, but also that most other people agree that they are right.† A line-up in a UN debate often

* Lady Violet Bonham Carter, at a lunch given for U Thant by the United Nations Association in London in July 1962.

† e.g. Khrushchev, on 10 July 1962, defending Soviet resumption of nuclear weapons tests: 'Anyone who follows world developments knows that the Soviet Union's rocket and nuclear strength is the decisive factor in preserving peace.' Or – a more sophisticated version – Home, on 13 July: 'What I want to know ... is what the majority of the Assembly, or rather the over-vocal minority ... dragging a great number of otherwise reasonable and friendly delegates in their wake, what these people want and what they think they are achieving.'

destroys such illusions; which can be irritating, but is salutary if one wants to stay in touch with reality. In the 1956 Suez conflict, many people in Britain preferred to think that only Dulles, Nehru, and Nasser's immediate friends were really against them; when an overwhelming Assembly majority demanded the withdrawal of the British, French, and Israeli troops from Egypt, this balloon of complacency was pricked. In September 1960, after Khrushchev had denounced Hammarskjöld as 'upholding the colonialists' interests' in the Congo, another huge majority, including all the Asian and African states swamped Russia's lonely opposition and carried an Afro-Asian resolution urging the Secretary-General to 'continue to take vigorous action'.

The talk-shop may be often tedious, occasionally silly, and, sometimes, it may seem that it is not even listening to itself (a misleading appearance; the content of a speech is often known beforehand, through consultations or the handing out of an advance text). But any government that does not bother to note the tone of UN debates is liable to get nasty surprises later on when it finds its policies running into unexpected opposition – and, equally, liable to miss opportunities to act in ways that will win it friends and good repute.

Could not a government get the same 'feel' of world opinion through the normal, discreet channels of diplomacy? Not, it seems, so fully. One reason is that many of the post-war world's small new states have only a limited diplomatic apparatus. The little republic of Anonymia cannot station in every other country's capital an ambassador with enough experience and skill to get across to that country's government the exact nuances of Anonymian opinion and its likely reactions to events. To a good many Anonymias, the UN is a focal-point of diplomacy. They send their best representatives there, because they can then keep in touch with many other governments – in particular, with the other little Anonymias. Little states cannot carry much weight in the world unless they align themselves with friends; so Anonymia's actual policy (as distinct from its mere aspirations) is largely shaped by the alignments that its man at the UN finds possible there. And bigger states can sometimes see the Anonymias more steadily, and see them more as a whole, when their representatives gather at Turtle Bay, than they could do merely on the basis of separate reports from their diplomats in all the Anonymias' capitals.

Could not the 'feel' be got, however, by informal contact at the UN, without all the speechmaking? Much of it is. And, in private talk, one delegate learns from another a great deal that never goes 'on the record' in public statements. But, although *tête-à-tête* conversation can clear a lot of ground, it is seldom possible to establish just how much agreement on an issue there is without getting together in larger numbers than twos. Some of these larger meetings are, of course, held in private, and it is often argued that more of them should be. The main arguments for closed meetings are that they prevent 'playing to the gallery', and thus reduce the amount of useless speechmaking (especially the bits that are really meant for the newspapers back home); and that they make for flexibility, as a delegate can withdraw from a position more easily if he has not got stuck with it in public. But this is an old controversy, and Robert Cecil's arguments against closed meetings, as valid now as in the League's day, are worth noting:

To withdraw from a position taken up in committee is not much less humiliating than if it had been adopted in open debate. ... Finally, the proceedings of an international committee are never really private. They are almost always reported. But, instead of there being one accurate report made by shorthand writers, there are a number of tendentious reports put out by zealous nationals. ...*

The deafening, deadening flood of oratory has, in the end, two practical sides to it. First, it lets off steam – sometimes spontaneously, sometimes with calculated intent.

A Great Experiment, page 92.

When a country's particular grievances have been vented
in a speech (perhaps during the 'general debate' – the
long, diffuse talkfest with which each Assembly begins;
perhaps by dragging them into a debate on some different
issue), it may feel less need to press for an actual vote on
them, in circumstances in which a vote will do no good
and may do it harm. And when a government knows that
its vote (or abstention) on an issue is going to offend
people (in the UN, or at home) with whom it does not
wish to quarrel, it can, through a speech, try to show that
it is more in sympathy with them than its vote suggests.

Secondly, speechmaking – especially, tedious speechmaking that nobody need really listen to – provides more
time for getting on with the real business.

Dean Rusk, long before he became Secretary of State,
but after having had personal experience as a UN delegate,
wrote that

there are times when United Nations debate – prolonged, boring,
discouraging – is in fact a sophisticated, useful, and often planned
device for finding time in which the fever can subside.*

This is an understatement. While the speeches surge and
thunder like ocean on a distant beach, the time they take
up is often being put to good use outside the debating
chambers in many ways, of which the bringing down of
fever is only one.

Sometimes the results, and the contrast between public
oratory and hidden activity, are dramatic. In December
1957 eight days of debate in committee on the war in
Algeria had produced apparent deadlock. An Assembly
committee can adopt a resolution by a simple majority. If
it is only a small majority, the resolution will not get
through the plenary session, in which a two to one majority
is needed, and will not go on record as an Assembly
decision; but when that happens there is a certain satisfaction both for those who supported the resolution and

* 'Parliamentary Diplomacy – Debate vs Negotiation', in *World
Affairs Interpreter*, Los Angeles, Summer 1955.

for those who opposed it. In the case of Algeria, however, even this proved impossible. The committee vote was an exact tie, thirty-seven to thirty-seven, the other eight members of a total of eighty-two abstaining.

On 10 December, with only four days to go to the scheduled closing of the Assembly – and delegates who, in that year of aftermath, had already sat from January to March in the wake of Suez, and met again in early September to look back in anger at Hungary, were un-usually eager to finish – Algeria came up in plenary, with no resolution forwarded from the committee at all. The ill-informed shuddered at the thought of the whole debate being gone through again, with no better prospect of agreement on anything. But the well-informed winked. Sir Leslie Munro of New Zealand, the Assembly's president, wasted no time that morning. Without inviting anybody to speak, he produced, like a rabbit from a hat, a draft resolution – a carefully phrased compromise text – which until that moment had not seen the light of day. It was carried by eighty votes to none, without debate, there and then.

Eisenhower, in his opening speech at the emergency Assembly on Lebanon and Jordan in August 1958, dwelt on what could be done to make the Arab deserts bloom by joint effort, and mentioned that underground rivers can now be traced by radio-active isotopes, and wells sunk in the right places to tap the flow far below the surface. His vision of economic cooperation in the Middle East faded like a mirage during the arid week of recriminatory speeches that followed. But through that week a political river, starting from a fountainhead designed by Ham-marskjöld (page 109), flowed strongly, out of sight, beneath the desert of oratory.

Abdul Khalik Hassouna, secretary-general of the Arab League, and Mohammed Mahgoub, foreign minister of Sudan, eventually got all the quarrelling Arab delegates into Hassouna's suite at the Hotel Pierre on Fifth Avenue on the evening of Tuesday, 19 August. On Wednesday afternoon all the Arabs circulated a joint draft resolution; on Thursday the Assembly adopted it unanimously and went home rejoicing. Very few observers had had the right isotopes to track the subterranean flow this time. Even the Arab Press had to eat its former harsh words overnight when the 'good neighbour' resolution suddenly gushed to the surface.

To see how such things can happen, we must leave the talk-shop proper, and go underground too.

OFF STAGE

Satow's Guide to Diplomatic Practice has nothing to say about corridors. Or about *coulisses* (which, strictly, means the wings, but is often equated with *couloirs*). Or about lobbies, lounges, bars, 'smoke-filled rooms', caucus rooms, and the other such places where, at Turtle Bay as elsewhere, diplomacy is mostly practised.

'The big glasshouse', as some call the UN building – although it is by no means the biggest of Manhattan's glass-walled citadels – rises on the edge of the East River rather like an iceberg upside down. Although it boasts three basement levels, there is more of it, architecturally speaking, above the surface than below. Politically, it is the other way round. Those glass walls are deceptive; you can see very little of what is really happening through them. John Hadwen and Johan Kaufmann, writing with experience as members of the Canadian and Netherlands UN missions behind them, go so far as to say that

most UN decisions are settled by informal negotiating processes outside the formal meetings. ... The UN visitor, therefore, hears, except in cases of major conflict, the public explanation of what has been agreed privately.*

'Fixing', horse-trading, arm-twisting, log-rolling – call them what you will, these off-stage processes are a vital

* *How United Nations Decisions are Made,* Sythoff, Leyden, and Oceana, New York, 1960; revised edition 1962.

part of the UN, as of every other political machine of a parliamentary or quasi-parliamentary kind. The UN might, at a pinch, get by without any speechmaking at all (or, to provide the necessary time for back-stage work, selected non-controversial oratory, pre-recorded in the Muzak manner, could perhaps be piped through the headphone systems in the conference chambers). But without the off-stage processes, it simply would not work. There is nothing necessarily sinister or even disreputable about these processes. What is 'fixed' behind the scenes has still to be confirmed publicly and formally. The fixers must, therefore, devise a proposal that will get the necessary majority when it comes to a formal vote.

In the 'corridors', the first rough draft of a resolution may be changed thirty or forty times as it goes the rounds, being shown privately to one delegation after another. Normally, its sponsors would not dream of presenting it officially until they are reasonably sure of majority backing. Sometimes even that is not enough: the aim may be not to win a bare victory, but to find a formula that practically every member can support.

Why, then, is any proposal ever publicly defeated at all, if so much care is taken to put up only certain winners? There are three main reasons. First, there is not always time for thorough canvassing. Secondly, some of those who are canvassed may hum and haw so evasively that not even the shrewdest judge of form can tell how they will vote when the moment comes, and the chance just has to be taken. Thirdly, some resolutions are publicly proposed in cold-blooded knowledge that they cannot possibly go through; their sponsors may count the loss of face well worth while, if the mere publication of their proposal embarrasses the champions of a rival plan and perhaps forces them to modify it.

Where and how all this lobbying is done depends on the time available, the numbers directly involved, and the need for discretion. Suppose that the governments of Anonymia, Synonymia, and Pseudonymia are set on pushing some important project through, but are in no great hurry. Their top Turtle Bay men, Ambassadors Anon, Syn, and Pseud,* with such allies as they can muster from the very start, may spend weeks patiently lunching, dining, and wining their prospective converts, working round to their theme very gently at the coffee-and-cognac stage, tackling the easier prospects in twos and threes and the stickier ones individually. This is the grand old diplomacy as everybody, including diplomats, likes to dream of it. But time is seldom so spaciously available.

Anon, Syn, and Pseud may have to catch their men practically on the wing, shoving their little bits of paper under their noses and pleading for a quick decision, while shifting from one tired foot to the other and aching for the end of a long day, or at least for a chance to get to the washroom and swallow another couple of aspirins. Aches and anxieties must not make them betray any tetchiness, or blur the nice points of their own formulas, or miss the nuances of anybody's reactions. Sometimes diplomats earn their *frais* most fully when their expenses (except on aspirin) are lowest.

Secrecy does not always matter. In fact, at times the originators of a move seek publicity from the start, especially if they think they have set rolling a bandwaggon that many others will be happy to jump on. But in many cases a decent discretion has to be observed, if only to avoid embarrassing delegates who may be being wooed by two or more rival groups and do not yet want to appear committed to any of them. If Anon undertakes to approach

* While these names are not meant to refer to actual persons, I apologize in advance to any delegate who may appear at Turtle Bay under one of them. The list of delegations has included Messrs Ba, Hu, Ng, Li, Lo, Ant, Nyi, Eno, Oto, Jha, Cha, Mod, Quao, Kit, Sow, Uys, and Zea; also (just to indicate the range) Eouagnignon, Kosciusko-Morizet, Pholphatphicharn, and W. F. McIlquham Schmidt. I would hesitate to invent a UN delegate called Mr X; there has already, I am told, been a real one named O, and an X may turn up anytime.

the Ruritanians, he must decide whether he will personally tackle his opposite number, Ambassador Rurit; whether it would be more discreet if the first move were made by his own junior colleague, An, having a word with Rurit's junior, Ru; whether Rurit (a touchy chap) might be offended if he did not get the word directly from Anon; and so on.

Some of the permutations involve personalities; if Ru is to be tackled, Pseud's junior, Pse, might be a better man than An to do it, not because An is incompetent but because the Pse and Ru families have been seeing a lot of each other and getting on well. But, again, time may be too pressing to work out an ideal plan of attack; in the end, it may largely depend on who gets stuck in crosstown traffic jams, who is sure to see whom at that morning's committee sessions, and who simply cannot be found at the crucial moment. To find somebody at short notice is not always easy.

The chances of catching people in the UN building depend on how well you know their likely movements. If your man is certain to be at a committee session or a caucus meeting about the time you want him, or if the times of his visits to the delegates' lounge for a drink at the bar or a cup of coffee are practically unvarying, then he is easily intercepted. Otherwise, a telephone call to his delegation's offices somewhere in midtown Manhattan may yield the unhelpful information that he, like you, is in the UN building, but nobody knows quite where. At peak periods, the loudspeakers emit a steady stream of plaintive requests for Ambassador Anon (or Mr Pse, or Mr Ru) to call the delegates' lounge, indicating that somebody has thus lost contact.

An occasional loss of contact is nothing, though; the UN building is a vast convenience when a diplomat has to make a whole series of contacts in quick succession. To do the same job in any of the world's capitals, he would have to shuttle madly to and fro between embassies, the foreign ministry, and appointments in restaurants and private homes. At Turtle Bay he can arrange most of his rendez-vous within the glass walls and save time and energy.

If Pse and Ru regularly attend the same committee, Pse can sell Ru his ideas in quiet talk actually in the committee room, while the speeches roll on regardless. If not, there are groups of comfortable chairs disposed at decent intervals along the corridors. If the Ruritanians are sympathetic to the project anyway, and merely need to be kept informed about its latest shape, a quick word at the bar, or on the hoof through the lobbies, may be enough. If they need more persuading lunch may be indicated – in the delegates' dining-room, or, if Pse cannot get a table there, or wants to show Ru some papers which he would rather not be seen passing round, across First Avenue at Ferdi's or farther afield in Manhattan.

Glass-walled though it is, the building is an easier place to negotiate in without being remarked than any other centre of diplomacy in the world. Suppose that Anonymia and Ruritania are in a state of strained relations. If Ambassador Anon, stationed in Ruritania's capital, is charged with offering a new formula for settling their differences, he may attract unwanted attention if he calls at the foreign ministry or invites one of its senior officials to a *téte-à-téte* meal. But at Turtle Bay he is continually thrown together with Rurit; and, if they are seen hob-nobbing, who can tell whether they are tackling their countries' mutual grievances, or merely dickering about some minor matter of UN procedure, such as who shall be the committee's next *rapporteur*? There is always some routine business – agenda priorities, elections to minor offices, the unravelling of procedural tangles – that provides an excuse for starting conversations.

There are often helpful intermediaries too. Neither Anon nor Rurit may be willing (or authorized) to approach the other directly with a view to settling their differences; but Syn, representing a government that would be much relieved if Anonymo-Ruritanian relations got better, will gladly serve as go-between, and, if both are agreeable will invite them to meet as his guests and gently probe the problem, Syn himself either taking part in the talk as a tactful host, or, with equal tact, leaving them by themselves for a while.

Syn's role at times falls to the Secretariat (see, for instance, page 113); at others, a joint move for conciliation may be made by both Secretariat and friendly delegations. With or without intermediaries, the mere fact of being brought together at the UN can make it easier for antagonists to get off their high horses. An outstanding case was the cordial meeting in 1960 between Macmillan and Nasser neither of whom was in a position to take the initiative in approaching the other. At Turtle Bay, these things can be managed.

When foreign ministers, presidents, and such are in town, their suites in the Waldorf Towers and similar high haunts naturally become nodal points in the cat's-cradle of diplomatic contacts. The corridors of the glasshouse then take second place in activity, though they buzz with more gossip than usual. But normally, when the great men are not around, the UN scene shows relatively little in the way of high life (except the dance of that name, at Ghanaian parties), or of social stratification. Inside the building most senior hierarchs unbend quite readily, and nervous new boys soon feel at home. Ambassadors extraordinary and plenipotentiary, young third secretaries, journalists and other ranks stand in line together to get a coffee and a sandwich in the main lounge, rub elbows at the bars, squeeze into lifts, and emerge from the committee rooms after long night sessions weary but with a certain sense of fellowship.*

The corporate spirit of 'the house' cannot, of course, overcome all barriers. Careful politeness is the most that

* If Turtle Bay has a *genus loci*, it ought to be an egalitarian one. It was peopled, before the UN moved in, by slaughtermen and bargees. That is why Tudor City, the group of tall residential blocks, with Hampton Court trimmings, just across First Avenue, coldly presents to the UN a blank face broken only by small bathroom windows.

can be expected between, say, Arabs and Israelis,* Soviet bloc delegates and Chinese Nationalists, Africans and South Africans. But some highly improbable personal friendships do develop, often as a result of a small group of assorted delegates being assigned to do some minor job together, and then, when the job is done, having to back each other up to prevent somebody else undoing it all.

Each such friendship is a diplomatic asset, as in the case of Pse and Ru. Especially when time is short, you can tackle your man to better effect if he is an old friend or, failing friendship, an old acquaintance; both of you will then be less liable to misunderstand what exactly the other is getting at.

A lot of lobby time is therefore spent in simply getting to know other people, and in keeping alive personal contacts that may come in handy some day. Newcomers need to learn their way round Turtle Bay's sea of faces as quickly as they can; old hands need to sort out the identities and idiosyncrasies of each new intake (quite a task in itself when, as in 1960, seventeen new delegations appear during one Assembly).

'The fine art of corridor sitting', as Marya Mannes once dubbed it in the *Reporter*, has more to it than is suggested by the sight of an outwardly relaxed delegate resting his backside in a vast chair in the lounge. You can't tell whom he may be hoping to ambush. Nor, sometimes, can he; but, as an experienced Bayman, he knows that, with an hour to fill between engagements, as good a use for the time as any is to sit and let the diplomatic world go by, collecting, perhaps, a new acquaintance or a bit of fresh information, trying out a balloon or two on any colleague who may stop for a moment, and, of course,

* For seven years, the alphabetical order had the Israeli member of each committee seated uncomfortably between an Iraqi and a Lebanese. New admissions – fortunately, just before Suez – introduced some 'buffer states'. Ireland and Italy now flank Israel, and the three of them relish the claim that, together, they constitute the delegation of New York City.

waiting to see if anything interesting will be tried out on himself.

Alfred Hitchcock once staged a murder (on film) in the main delegates' lounge. His craftsman's eye must have seen at first glance the dramatic qualities of this huge but comfortable and club-like room, the East River pictured in the windows that reach to its lofty ceiling, the cosiness of a little coffee-shop skilfully achieved in the enclave at the far end, behind the L-shaped bar.

Some tendency to homicide may, indeed, lurk behind the mass blandness of a crowd of diplomats. But if murder *is* ever done here, it will surely have a personal rather than a political motive. Political antagonists at the UN, however furious their rhetorical jousts, show little venom once the debate is over. Flashes of real bitterness are more often to be detected when there is personal rivalry over a committee chairmanship or some other elective post. Heated charges of 'fixing' or 'log-rolling' may then be heard on the lips of delegates whose own duties largely consist of those very activities.

The outsider, puzzled by this pettiness, has to remind himself that professional ambition is a useful driving-force, without which it might be hard to get anybody into the somewhat frustrating career of diplomacy at all. He will note, at the same time, that he hears little griping about such matters from delegates who are most directly involved in the more constructive work of the UN. They are not necessarily too pure in spirit to be envious, but they are often too busy.

BLOCS AND THE BRIGADE

What is a bloc? One answer is: when it's against you. The North Atlantic allies are invariably a 'bloc', and an aggressive bloc at that, in Soviet statements; in which statements, what we know as the Soviet bloc is termed a camp, or – bringing a blush to British cheeks – a Commonwealth. When non-aligned countries get together (to seek alignment with one another), they denounce 'both blocs' and recoil, shuddering, from any idea that they constitute a bloc themselves. It is, after all, a four-letter word.

If one tries to use the word unemotionally and precisely, as meaning a group of states that act in disciplined unison, then there is only one bloc in the UN: the Soviet bloc. There are chips off even this bloc. Poland has veered, slightly but perceptibly, toward one deviation; Albania (since 1960) rather more perceptibly toward another. But to see the chips (as distinct from the great gash where Yugoslavia broke off in 1948) has required a close look.

It might be very different if China were represented in the UN by its Communist government, instead of by Nationalists from Formosa. Communist China, for instance, openly denounced the UN decision to launch the Congo operation – a decision for which Russia had voted. Up to 1963, however, the members of the bloc took the Russian whip in every UN vote. Occasionally one, mistaking the signals, voted the wrong way – correcting itself as soon as it saw how Moscow's man had voted.*

But the Soviet bloc accounts for only a tenth of the UN's membership. The other nine-tenths show far less discipline. As Sydney Bailey has written in an admirably careful study, 'The outstanding fact . . . is the tendency of member states to affiliate differently for different purposes.'†

The result is a pattern of voting so complex that only a three-dimensional figure in rainbow colours could show it adequately. I once took, as a random sample, a mere four Assembly votes, taken within a few days of each other. The Arab states alone showed six different voting records in this small sample. The Asian states also showed six different records; so did the non-Arab Africans; the West Europeans divided up seven ways. Five of the NATO allies voted differently from America; so did several Latin-Americans;

---

* Late in 1963, Rumania caused excitement by stepping out of line in a single vote on a secondary issue; the exception proved the rule.

† *The General Assembly of the United Nations*, Stevens, London, and Praeger, New York, 1960.

and all the ex-French African republics voted differently from France on one or more of the four issues.

Altogether, the members of what is so often called the 'Afro-Asian bloc' showed no less than thirteen different voting patterns on these four issues alone; on one issue, as many as twenty-two of them voted the same way as America and Britain; on another, as many as eighteen the same way as Russia. India, Nigeria, Ghana, and the United Arab Republic voted together on all four issues, but only seven other Afro-Asians followed their lead.

Bailey prefers to apply the word 'bloc' only to Russia's team, and then to distinguish two kinds of looser association between UN members: the temporary coalitions formed for a special purpose, and the established groups which periodically meet, consult, and arrange certain matters between themselves, but do not necessarily act in unison. Hadwen and Kaufmann (already quoted on page 64) use 'bloc' more loosely, but agree that 'divisions run through almost all the blocs'. So do other close observers of the UN, including H. G. Nicholas, who has dealt firmly with what he calls 'the exaggerated concern over bloc voting'.* All informed commentators point out that an organization of so many separate sovereign members could hardly be workable at all without some kind of grouping.

Nicholas's book brings out a particular paradox in British criticism of the UN. On the one hand it is often held that all 'blocs' are sinful, that each member should vote uncompromisingly according to his own conscience. On the other, the British are used to firm parliamentary alignments at home, and the loose ways of Turtle Bay often evoke 'the plaintive cry of the M.P. on the British delegation, "*Where* is the discipline?"'

As Nicholas shows, any attempt to understand the UN Assembly in terms of the House of Commons is hopeless. It is more easily interpreted in terms of the Trade Union Congress, or of an American party convention, in which

* *The United Nations as a Political Institution*, Oxford University Press, 1959.

there is no disciplined majority but a set of 'constituent parts that are frequently older, prouder, and more tenacious than the whole'; in which the only way to get results is to form alliances, by trading votes, threats, and promises, and by shaping policies with a broad appeal.

It is widely assumed that throughout the UN's first decade there was an automatic Assembly majority at the disposal of America, and that there is now one controlled by the Afro-Asian members. Both these generalizations are over-simplified. In the early years, when total membership grew slowly from fifty-one to sixty, there were twenty Latin-American and fifteen other 'Western' (NATO and 'old Commonwealth') votes available to put through any resolution that the Western countries were really agreed about. Yet, even in those days, America could not count on all these votes being automatically available; sometimes it could not whip them all in even when it chose to use strong pressure (usually by economic inducements).

A vivid example was the Assembly resolution on partitioning Palestine in November 1947. America was lobbying intensively for this resolution. (Russia and France also backed it, and Secretary-General Trygve Lie was working hard for it too.) Yet Bernard Moore records that only a few days before the final vote the necessary majority of two to one was not in sight. The Assembly then took a break for Thanksgiving Day:

> The traditional American dish on this day is roast turkey; and, as one cynical observer put it, on that Thanksgiving Day American embassies in some of the smaller countries talked turkey in real earnest.*

When the debate was resumed, several members switched to support the resolution, and it was carried. But even under this exceptional pressure, only thirteen of the twenty Latin-Americans voted for it.

America's success in keeping the Peking government out of the Chinese seat at the UN has long been regarded

* *The Second Lesson*, Macmillan, London, 1957.

as a yardstick of American influence. Peking can hardly
be kept out for ever; but what is surely remarkable is that
as late as October 1963 only forty-one votes out of 111
were cast in favour of seating its representatives. Only
twenty-five Asian and African states voted in favour;
twenty-three of them voted against, and six abstained.
This scarcely fits the prevalent idea that the Assembly
has now been 'captured' by a massive Afro-Asian 'bloc',
single-mindedly anti-western and easily manipulated by
the Communist powers.

The nearest thing to a clear picture of Afro-Asian
dominance that the Assembly has yet seen was, perhaps,
its vote of censure on a speech made to it by South
Africa's foreign minister in October 1961. Even then, the
sixty-seven who voted for censure did not include all the
Asians, but did include sixteen states that were neither
Asian, African, nor Communist. More significant was the
fact that South Africa was alone in voting against; not
even Portugal joined it.

Much more typical, in recent Assembly line-ups on
questions of colonialism and racialism, have been thumping
majorities of ninety or more, in which a good many West
European countries, America, and the older Commonwealth countries have joined. The resolution of November
1961 calling for a rapid end to colonialism was carried by
ninety-seven to nil, with only Britain, France, Portugal,
South Africa, and Spain abstaining. By this test it would
seem that the 'anti-colonial bloc' in the UN comprises all
but a small minority of the members.

It cannot even be shown that the Afro-Asians are a
rabidly extreme element within this huge majority group.
On the contrary, in most debates on colonial issues it has
been a common practice for them to turn a cold shoulder
to Russia's proposals (many of which have been withdrawn
for lack of support), and to put forward less extreme
drafts of their own. Repeatedly, they have also preferred
the more moderate of the various proposals put up within
their own ranks. For instance, the 1961 Assembly, which

voted ninety-seven to two for a resolution condemning
South Africa's racialism and urging it to change its ways,
was also offered a tougher resolution calling for direct
action against South Africa; but this proposal, mainly
backed by Africans, was cold-shouldered by a dozen
Asian states and failed to go through. An immoderate
resolution on Oman put up by Arab states in 1961 was
backed by less than half of the Afro-Asians, and likewise
failed; but the Arabs' resolution on Algeria, couched in
restrained terms, went through without a single dissentient
vote. There is a premium on moderation; and no Afro-Asian
state can put up any old resolution in an anti-colonial
vein in confidence that the whole group will back it.

The belief that the Asians and Africans constitute a
'bloc' partly arises from the fact that their group holds
regular private meetings – every week or two when the
Assembly is in session – and nominates candidates for
election to the Security Council, to the Assembly's steering
committee, and to other bodies. So do the Latin-Americans,
and the Commonwealth countries. These group meetings
are not caucuses in the true sense. They do not decide
questions by voting and then make the group decision
binding on all members. They seek agreement when it is
possible, and, if it is not, understanding. The meetings are
informal and off the record; but inevitably a good deal
leaks out.

The Latin-American group is the most formalized; it
dates from League days, and operated from the very start
of the UN, of which all twenty Latin-American republics
were founder members. They are not always agreed even
on issues, such as anti-colonialism, which in principle
they all support. Portugal used to be able to count on a
good deal of sympathy from its fellow Latins, until the
carnage in Angola in 1961 turned many of their stomachs.
Some of the little Central American 'banana republics'
have earned notoriety as ever-willing echoes of the United
States; but, even before Castro brought Cuba to a position
of bitter hostility to the U.S.A., there was a fairly wide

range of Latin-American deviation from Washington's policies. The group has maintained its solidarity most consistently in jointly putting forward candidates for election to UN posts of all kinds. By thus holding together, it has, for example, kept two of the six elective seats in the Security Council for Latin-Americans – a disproportionately large share now that the Latins fill less than a fifth of the Assembly, as against their two fifths in 1945.

The Afro-Asian group, although similarly equipped with chairmen, spokesmen, and regular meetings, is really more of an umbrella covering several overlapping sub-groups. The main group dates from 1950, when six Arab and six Asian delegations began to consult together. Its first non-Arab African members, Ethiopia and Liberia, joined it in 1955, the year of the Afro-Asian conference at Bandung. Today, 'black Africa' provides half of its unwieldily swollen membership of over fifty.

The thirteen Arab states make up its oldest sub-group. All of them belong to the Arab League, founded in 1945, whose office in New York is a rallying point even when the Arabs are quarrelling, and whose secretary-general has been an authorized observer at UN Assemblies since 1950. They have seldom been free from disputes among themselves. Iraq was at odds with Egypt both before and after its 1958 revolution; in 1961, when Iraq was seeking to annex Kuwait, Egypt sponsored Kuwait's application to join the UN (which Russia vetoed). The 1958 Arab crisis (page 110) ended in a hollow reconciliation, Jordan in particular remaining under pressure from its neighbours; later there were open quarrels between Tunisia and Egypt, Egypt and Saudia Arabia, Saudi Arabia and Iraq. Syria and Egypt formed the United Arab Republic in 1958, but broke up in 1961, the name of the U.A.R. being retained by Egypt alone; in 1963 the plan to federate these two and also Iraq (and possibly Yemen) was set back when fresh quarrels erupted. But the Arabs have worked together over these years in sponsoring at the UN the cases of the Algerians against France, of the Omanis in revolt against the British-protected Sultan of Muscat, and of the Palestine Arabs against Israel. A Palestine Arab, Ahmed Shukairy, once attached to the Syrian delegation and later Saudi Arabia's permanent UN representative, in a sense personifies both the Arabs' basic solidarity and their differences; his bitter oratory has often embarrassed his colleagues.

In 1958 the five Arab African states (Egypt, Libya, Morocco, Sudan, Tunisia) joined with Ethiopia, Ghana, Guinea, and Liberia – at that time the only independent African states south of the Sahara – to form the UN's first African sub-group, which for three years held its own private meetings and was served by a joint secretariat. But by 1961 there had occurred not only a massive admission of new African UN members, but also the split between the 'Casablanca' states – Egypt, Ghana, Guinea, Mali, Morocco, and the Algerians, then still in exile – and the less radical 'Monrovia' grouping of twenty-one African states, including the twelve ex-French republics often known as the 'Brazzaville' states. (All these names are derived from places where the groups held their formative conferences.) Reconciliation between 'Casablancans' and 'Monrovians' came easier after Algeria won its independence in 1962 and UN action disposed of the Tshombe régime in the Katanga early in 1963. At their Addis Ababa conference in May 1963 the 32 African governments made common cause with the aim of ending white domination in the south. Yet various local quarrels, and apparent shifts of alignment, persisted.

The Belgrade conference of non-aligned states in 1961 had overlaid these patterns with another. Except for Yugoslavia, Cyprus, and Cuba, it was an Afro-Asian affair, attended by all the Arabs, by Ethiopia, Ghana, Guinea, Mali, and the Congo (represented by both Adoula and Gizenga), and by India and six other Asian states. The differences revealed at a gathering whose purpose was to emphasize unity, and from which there were significant absences, illustrated the problem of maintaining a consistently united front in the larger Afro-Asian group at the UN. Perhaps the one safe generalization to be made about the whole group – it is a risky game to label each of these states as really 'left' or 'right', 'moderate', 'pro-Western', or 'pro-Soviet' – is that its members, while they still have a lot to learn about how to use the UN to good effect, are increasingly aware of the importance to them of the UN's continued development.

The Commonwealth group now overlaps extensively with the Afro-Asian: eleven of its eighteen members (in early 1964) are Asian or Africans. It is, of course, even less like a 'bloc' than the other groups. Historically, it is now worth recalling that in the League's Assembly (at least in the eyes of some American commentators) 'the most powerful and united group was that composed of Great Britain and the Dominions'.* Although the British may thus have been the pioneers of blocmanship, the Commonwealth group in the UN was notable for lack of unity even in the first post-war years, long before the great inrush of new members. In 1947, for example, Canada, Australia, New Zealand, and South Africa voted for Palestine partition; India and Pakistan voted against; and Britain abstained. Even while India was still under British tutelage, it appealed to the Assembly in 1946 about South Africa's treatment of Indians. From 1948 on, India and Pakistan were embroiled over Kashmir, still one of the UN's recurring headaches today. In 1956 the Asian countries were outraged by the British attack on Egypt; Australia and New Zealand backed Britain; Canada publicly deplored the British action and took a leading part in creating the UN force to hasten withdrawal (page 105); South Africa, already in strained relations with the Assembly, held aloof.

Through all such storms and stresses, the Commonwealth group in the UN has continued to consult together regularly, its value as a bridge of personal contact and at least partial understanding actually increasing as the

* Daniel S. Cheever and H. Field Haviland, *Organising for Peace*, Houghton Mifflin, Boston, and Stevens, London, 1954.

gulfs to be bridged have widened. It has been said that Commonwealth countries have often led both the right wing and the left wing in the UN – particularly in the context of southern Africa. One might add that some of them have played a constructive role in the centre.

In spite of the transforming of the group by the entry of the Asian and African members, it has maintained a certain continuity in its UN role. Now, as in 1945, it embraces one of the five veto-wielding Council members, and a number of 'smaller nations' of which, however, several are better classed as 'middle powers' since they stand out from the ruck both by their physical proportions, and by their readiness to challenge the great powers and to offer positive leadership in the development of the UN.

At San Francisco, while the Charter was still being thrashed out, Herbert Evatt of Australia and Peter Fraser of New Zealand spearheaded the struggle to reduce the privileges that the great powers planned to assign themselves. By an understanding reached in 1946, one elective Council seat was earmarked for the Commonwealth, and this claim has so far held good, Australia, Canada, New Zealand, India, Pakistan, Ceylon, and Ghana having all taken a turn. Five Assemblies have had Commonwealth presidents – Evatt, Lester Pearson of Canada, Vijayalakshmi Pandit of India, Munro of New Zealand, Zafrulla Khan of Pakistan. In general, the Commonwealth countries carry more than average weight in the UN. India is far the largest state in non-Communist Asia. Pakistan is linked not only with the West by alliances but also, as an Islamic republic, with the Arab world (it has been a vigorous champion of Algerian independence). Nigeria is Africa's largest state; Ghana was the first of the new independent states of non-Arab Africa; Tanganyika occupies a key position in East Africa. Canada, Australia, and New Zealand, although members of Western alliances, are free enough from the taint of 'imperialism' to be often acceptable to Asian and African opinion as providers of UN

representatives in various capacities. Canada in particular
has a record of valuable bridgework between the West
and the Afro-Asian world.

The way Pearson virtually invented the UN force in
1956 was a spectacular example of this kind of constructive
work. In those days, Canadians at the UN used to call
themselves 'displaced Scandinavians'. There was much
more to this than the teamwork between Pearson, Hammarskjöld, and Hans Engen of Norway in the shaping of
the emergency force. The reference was to what *The
Economist* of 16 March 1957 called

the activity within the UN of a ginger group – a group of members
of more than negligible weight, with enough detachment to win
widespread confidence, enough concern for the general good to
break out of the parochial pattern of geographical blocs, enough
imagination to put forward new techniques, and enough gener-
osity to set an example by contributing physically to the development of those techniques.... The ginger group is not confined
to 'uncommitted' countries.... Canada and the Scandinavian
countries at present provide it with a hard core, not only as
contributors to the UN force but also as independent-minded
advocates of constructive sanity.... At the moment, there are
not enough Scandinavians to go round.

By the end of 1957, the same journal was thankfully
noting an 'undertow of realism, of preference for compromise rather than what the Secretary-General has
called illusory voting victories' in the Assembly; and
giving most of the credit to

the 'greater Scandinavia' group, the voluntary fire brigade of
delegates ... dedicated to the proposition that it would be a
pity if the United Nations tore itself to pieces for no particular
purpose. ...

The unwearying activity of the fire brigade ... is now the
most absorbing feature of UN sessions.... It is based on a
nucleus of nations that are not too deeply committed on colonial
and similar issues, but it represents a new working group of
'middle powers'.

Two years later *The Economist*, welcoming Irish initiatives at the 1959 Assembly, was pointing out that although 'many of the newer member states have rallied to help the by now old established fire brigade' in easing the Assembly out of deadlocks, moderation was liable to 'slide imperceptibly into inertia'; and that

> somebody has to keep the sluggish monster of Turtle Bay from lying down in its tracks. As well as Scandinavians to coax, it needs more honorary Irish to goad.

Joseph Lash has described 'the fire brigades – the groups of middle-sized powers led by Canada, Norway, India, Ireland, Tunisia, Nigeria, Yugoslavia, and Mexico' as embodying a shift of power in the Assembly, 'on many issues, to a kind of centre party'.* Hadwen and Kaufmann discuss the work of UN 'fire brigades' in the more limited sense of 'compromisers'. Sydney Bailey, on the other hand, writes of the 'moderate leadership' provided by

> a nucleus of countries.... The nucleus varies ... but countries like Brazil, Canada, India, Ireland, Mexico, Norway, Sweden, and Yugoslavia have provided a focus of leadership on some of the more difficult issues.

Bailey adds that their activity in the Assembly

> has, at times, been vital; but it has inevitably been sporadic. The only continuing source of leadership has been the Secretariat.

And Lash defines the fire brigades as the states that 'worked with the thirty-eighth floor'. Thus we come back to the pattern of partnership between the more constructively-minded smaller nations and the Secretariat: partnership not only in executing the intent of a general UN consensus, as already noted (page 47), but also in actually shaping that consensus; and shaping it not merely by finding lowest-common-denominator compromises between antagonistic groups, but also by devising bases for positive action.

* *Dag Hammarskjöld*, Doubleday, New York, 1961; Cassell, London, 1962.

5 · *Tough at the Top*

HIGH in the sky over Turtle Bay, on the thirty-eighth floor of the UN building, the Secretary-General's office – nothing above it but lift-cages, water tanks, and a ping-pong room – is suggestive of lofty detachment. From its windows, the East River barge traffic looks like a procession of water beetles; beyond the water, the roaring bustle of New York's Long Island boroughs is reduced to a toyland world. Thick carpets and muted typewriters make the thirty-eighth floor a still place – the more so to a visitor whom the fast elevators have just lifted out of the throng of the Assembly corridors far below on a busy day. In this high hush, it is natural at first to feel that here one is a bit out of this world; and it can be positively re-assuring to find one of the Secretary-General's closest associates in his braces and a tearing hurry.

'The most impossible job in the world', as Trygve Lie ruefully described it when handing over to Dag Hammarskjöld in 1953, may have an ivory-tower setting; but the setting is deceptive. The world presses in upon the occupant of these quiet chambers from every side, and the office lays upon the man a gruelling and dangerous burden.

Undoubtedly the holders of the office have brought much of this upon themselves by progressively enlarging its responsibilities, by choosing to 'live dangerously'. To have taken refuge in the idea that the job should be really no more than that of a chief clerk would have made for a quieter life. But there is equally little doubt that such a course would have barred the effective development of the United Nations.

The job, whether or not the most impossible, is probably the least understood in the world. Myths grow up around it like weeds. Many of them are flatly contradictory. Today, a prevalent belief is that the secretary-generalship was a mere cipher until Hammarskjöld breathed life into it. It needs recalling that he was originally held to be acceptable, in 1953, as a quiet, 'safe' man unlikely to run into the kind of antagonism that Lie's vigorous actions had aroused.

Hammarskjöld's achievement needs no exaggeration; it is impressive enough as it stands. The growth of the powers of the office was well under way before he took over. Lie's contribution to that growth deserves to be rescued from oblivion.

When Trygve Lie, former foreign minister of Norway, became the first UN Secretary-General in February 1946, he had to start not only from scratch, but under a handicap too. The handicap was the precedent of restraint set by the Secretaries-General of the League of Nations.

What pre-war precedent there was for an active political executive derived not from the League, but from the International Labour Organization, and in particular from its first Director, the French journalist Albert Thomas. Although Thomas had been launched with no more definite constitutional powers than the League Secretary-General, he developed a role of energetic leadership, and visibly relished the buffets it brought him. He was not inhibited from placing firm proposals of his own before the ILO conferences; he used his annual reports to make forceful pronouncements; he travelled widely and spoke his mind as he went. But the League record shows nothing of the kind.

Before the League was formed, debate had ranged widely about the authority that might be given to its chief executive officer. At one extreme, Sir Maurice Hankey (himself, at one point, a prospective first Secretary-General) proposed that the post should be merely a supervisory one, and that the secretariat should consist of national units, each headed by a national secretary. At the other, Robert Cecil urged at an early stage that the League should have a Chancellor, with independent powers to match this resounding title. The Greek statesman Eleutherios

Venizelos was actually sounded to see if he would accept such a post. When Venizelos declined, the drafters of the Covenant lost little time in cutting the job down to an essentially administrative one.

Sir Eric Drummond (later Lord Perth), the League's Secretary-General throughout its first thirteen years, took office, therefore, without any assigned political role at all. It was not even specified that his staff should have an international character. The existing precedents, in 1920, pointed to a League Secretariat put together, as in the staffing of various international conferences and bureaux, entirely from groups of officials in the service of national governments. The League Covenant contained nothing like the UN Charter's clear rule that a Secretariat official must owe loyalty only to the organization, and must neither seek nor accept instructions from his own government. Drummond's achievement was to create something quite new, a genuinely international Civil Service. The principle of its international loyalty was later laid down in staff regulations, in terms that were to be copied in the Charter's Article 100.

Drummond was a Whitehall man to the core, strong in the belief that a Civil Service 'had to be "politically celibate" (though not perhaps politically virgin)'.* When asked for advice, privately, he would give it, often to some effect; but even behind the scenes he would never do anything that might annoy one of the parties to a dispute. His public utterances were rare, formal, and discreet. He showed no wish to enlarge either the authority or the public image of his office. He never addressed the Assembly at all.

If his temperament had been of another sort, he might have made a bolder mark. The setting in which he worked was not wholly restrictive. The 1920 Assembly adopted a report declaring it his duty to inform the Council if 'in

* Hammarskjöld's description of this phase, in his Oxford lecture of 30 May 1961 on 'The International Civil Servant in Law and in Fact' (published by the Oxford University Press).

his opinion' a state was violating the Covenant. The 1921 Assembly went further, requiring him to report any 'danger' of a violation, and proposing that, whenever he so reported, 'the Council will meet'. Article 99 (see page 97) of the UN Charter scarcely goes any further than this; and it is Article 99 which is generally cited as clear proof that the UN Secretary-General has a legitimate political role.

Drummond let this instrument for the enlargement of his own office's authority rust unused. There is a recurrent legend that he summoned the Council himself in 1925 to secure a cease-fire between Greece and Bulgaria. In fact the summons, and the message calling for a cease-fire, went out in the name and under the authority of Aristide Briand, then foreign minister of France and president of the League's Council. The drafts prepared by Drummond in Geneva were approved by Briand over the telephone from Paris.*

Joseph Avenol, who succeeded Drummond in 1933 after serving as his deputy, sought a rather more active political role, but without success. The nations were now turning away from the League; and Avenol, a former French inspector-general of finance, was no Albert Thomas. He ran into trouble in 1936, when he went to see Mussolini in hope of finding a compromise that would bring Italy back to the League without the League formally recognizing its conquest of Ethiopia. Later, he blamed the Council for not backing up this move, which he regarded as a bid to keep Mussolini out of Hitler's embrace.

As war drew near, Avenol, sure that the League's political life was over, concentrated on salvaging its economic and social machinery. After the fall of France he resigned in a mood of despair, and offered his services to the Vichy government. Sean Lester, his deputy, an Irish diplomat, took over and saw the vestigial Secretariat through the war years.

* There are odd inconsistencies in some published accounts of this affair.

Trygve Lie's period of service had a background of rapidly worsening international relations that resembled Avenol's time more than Drummond's. Disenchantment came much more quickly after the Second World War than after the First. Lie was confronted with the first onset of the 'cold war', with the Berlin blockade of 1948–9, the deadlock over China and consequent Soviet boycott of the Council in early 1950, and then the Korean war. He left office before the Korean armistice, before Stalin's death had given any encouragement to hopes of a 'thaw' in Russia, and while McCarthyism was at its height in America.

In these years of stiffening deadlock and mounting tension, Lie fought hard against a trend to which a lesser man might have tamely resigned himself. His reputation has suffered for the obvious reason that some of the most conspicuous of his ventures failed. Was some element of pure bad luck involved? The record of his effort in 1950 to switch the China seat in the UN and thus get the Russians back into the Council strongly suggests that he might just have pulled it off, if the interval between the Communist victory in China and the invasion of South Korea had been even a few weeks longer (page 93).

He certainly lacked Hammarskjöld's fine hand; and he aimed higher than a Hammarskjöld in plunging more boldly into areas of direct conflict between the great powers. It must be recalled, however, that he had to operate in a UN which was still very much an 'East-West' structure; the 'third world' of the new nations, which was later to strengthen Hammarskjöld much as the trade-union element in the ILO had strengthened Thomas, was then only emerging (and Lie did not fully grasp its significance). And he had to begin by building on foundations of authority that were scarcely visible.

When he took office, he did not even have an established right to speak in Assembly or Security Council; except when reporting to the Council a potential threat to peace, in accordance with Article 99.

Before he left, Lie had won the right not merely to speak but to make major political proposals in public as well as in private; to table resolutions; to send out a mission of inquiry, even when the Council had been unable to agree to authorize one; to send envoys, or go in person, to beard ministers in their own capitals and urge them to change their policies; to criticize member governments publicly; to expose falsehoods in their delegates' statements on the floor of the Assembly; to demand speedy action from the Council, to its face, and without resort to Article 99. A busy team of contact men was making sure that governments knew his views on controversial issues, and often pressing them persistently.

He had had to fight from the very beginning of his campaign to establish what he was later to describe candidly as 'the series of precedents by which I had carefully sought, stage by stage, to build up the influence and prestige of the Secretary-General'.*

One day in April 1946, Lie intercepted the then president of the Security Council, Quo Tai-chi of China, just as he was entering the Council chamber, and tried to give him a paper stating his views of the legal aspects of the question to be discussed, which was whether to drop the case of Russia's failure to withdraw its army from Iran.

Quo was visibly put out. He would not take the paper. Lie, undeterred, handed it to one of his staff to pass to Quo, and sat down in his own place at the Council table; thinking hard, as he recalled later. This was his first assertion of a right to intervene in the Council. He had not meant to take Quo by surprise. The memorandum had been drafted only that morning, and he had simply been unable to contact Quo until they met in the doorway. But he did mean to press his claim. He decided that if Quo was going to ignore the paper he would have to push a bit harder than he had wished to, this first time round, and demand to be allowed to read it into the record himself.

* Trygve Lie, *In the Cause of Peace*, Macmillan, London, 1954.

Quo, too, had thought again. He had the memorandum read out. But he then proposed to set it aside and have an immediate vote on the Iran item. There followed a remarkable wrangle.

Lie's paper, although couched in legal forms, pointed in a political direction that happened to please Russia (and France) but not America. (Secretary of State Byrnes later told a Press conference that Lie had exceeded his powers by merely presenting the paper.)

It thus happened that the enlargement of the role of the Secretary-General was backed at its very start by none other than Andrey Gromyko, later to become Soviet foreign minister. Gromyko cited Article 99 to buttress Lie's claim, and declared that 'the Secretary-General has all the more right, and an even greater obligation, to make statements on various aspects of the questions considered by the Security Council'.

Perspective suggests that it was a fortunate chance in 1946 that Lie – largely because of his position in the matter of Iran – was rather doubtfully regarded in Washington, and that much less suspect in Moscow.

In September Gromyko opened another door for him. America had proposed that the Council send a mission of inquiry to the Greek frontier. Russia had indicated that it would veto the move. Lie, by now firing on all cylinders, promptly reserved his own 'right to make such inquiries or investigations as he may think necessary', if the American move was vetoed.

He pointed out that, if he was to do his duty under Article 99, he must be able to get the facts about a reportedly dangerous situation. He met no challenge – although he was in effect claiming that he was free, absolutely free, to do what the Council could be prevented from doing by a veto. And Gromyko sped him on his way:

I think Mr Lie was right in raising the question of his rights. . . . In this case, as in all other cases, the Secretary-General must act.

There is other evidence that the Russians, in these early

days, thought that a UN chief executive with fairly wide powers would be a useful moderator of Western predominance. They were later to regret helping to enlarge his powers.

The British, in Lie's time, were regarded by most people in the UN orbit as the really consistent opponents of any enlargement of his political role. This British attitude is often wrongly thought to have arisen from Lie's energetic tangling with the Palestine problem in 1947–8. In fact it existed from the start.

Both the UN's Scandinavian Secretaries-General began their service with a particular feeling of closeness to Britain, and ended with a puzzled sense of distance. Lie had worked in exile in London from 1940 to 1945. With his solid Social Democratic and trade-union background, he was mystified at the very start by finding America and Russia thrusting him upon an unenthusiastic British Labour government. (It was the last of the 'Big Five' to agree to his nomination, doing so only on the morning of the day on which the Council unanimously sponsored him.) In 1950 he found the British infuriatingly vacillating about the extension of his term. Of this he later wrote: 'I was angry with myself for having been led on, and angry with others for having led me on.'

It is hardly necessary to recall the British indignation that was heaped upon Hammarskjöld at the time of the Suez conflict, and the revival of similar passions by the Katanga fighting that led to his death. Yet, paradoxically, he regarded himself as building upon basic principles derived very largely from Britain – the principles of a non-partisan Civil Service with a single loyalty; although he was fully – one might say by the end painfully – aware of the characteristic British recoil from all idea of Civil Servants interpreting their mandate in a way that suggested the taking of political decisions.

Undoubtedly, the Palestine conflicts increased London's mistrust of the growing activity of the Secretary-General.

Lie never concealed his position on Palestine. From the moment the UN special committee (UNSCOP) came out in favour of partition by a majority of seven to three in 1947, he urged support for the partition plan, which the Assembly adopted that November after what Lie described as 'an epic struggle'. He prodded the Council, both privately and publicly, for firm action to carry the decision through. When full-scale hostilities began, he dispatched special envoys – Andrew Cordier to Washington, Robert Jackson to London – to press for unity in upholding the UN's authority. He shouldered the Arab governments' anger philosophically.

At least the British position was consistently nihilist. Britain, having dumped Palestine on the UN, showed from the start that it did not like the UN plan and would not help to carry it out. America and Russia, together, rammed it through the Assembly. America then vacillated wildly. Lie told Warren Austin, America's UN representative, that they ought both to resign. Gromyko urged Lie not to; but it was Russia that then rejected categorically Lie's appeals, after the murder of the first UN mediator in Palestine, Bernadotte of Sweden, for a UN force of a few thousand men to check the bloodshed.

For the first time, a Secretary-General thus found that the great powers responsible for saddling the UN with a decision that required strong executive action were ratting on it – and on him – once things got really nasty.

Lie's discreeter role in the 1948–9 Berlin crisis was not a timid drawing back after his Palestine experience. The circumstances were quite different. Berlin was not thrust upon the UN as Palestine had been. It was a direct clash between the great powers; and they had reserved for themselves, in Article 107 of the Charter, a more or less free hand in German affairs. The UN role was necessarily a restricted one.

Philip Jessup, one of America's UN representatives, and

Dean Rusk, then head of the State Department's UN
section, asked Lie in October 1948 if he could help to
break the deadlock. Lie's behind-the-scenes efforts to that
end were given some encouragement by Russia, none by
Britain. He ran into American criticism when he agreed
to join Herbert Evatt of Australia, then president of the
Assembly, in an appeal for a great-power 'summit'
meeting; in doing so, he had certainly departed from his
original search for procedures which would not require
the West to negotiate publicly under the duress of the
blockade.

Much more serious American criticism was evoked
when Lie began, in January 1950, to work for the acceptance of the new Peking government by the UN. Once
again, this was an area of direct great-power conflict – an
area which Hammarskjöld never entered.

Lie argued, publicly and before American audiences,
that China had to be represented in the UN by the government that actually controlled it. At the same time he
publicly criticized Russia for boycotting UN meetings
while the Nationalists still occupied China's seat, and
pointed out that this flouted the rule of continuous attendance at the Security Council. Naturally, his prime
concern was to break a deadlock which had contributed to
an almost complete loss of contact between the powers; an
'impossible situation', he called it.

Before Yakov Malik walked out of the Council on 13
January – not to return until August – Ernest Gross had
told it that America would accept the seating of Peking's
men if any seven of the eleven Council members voted for
it. At the time, five of the eleven – Britain, India, Norway,
Russia, and Yugoslavia – recognized Peking. Lie went
the rounds of the members, armed with a memorandum
drawn up by his chief legal advisers – Ivan Kerno, a
League Secretariat veteran and friend of Jan Masaryk
who chose to remain in America after the Communist
putsch in his native Czechoslovakia, and Abraham Feller, one
of Lie's closest American friends, who was to kill himself in

1952 under the strain of the McCarthyite smear campaigns.*

There is evidence that his efforts helped to bring France close to the point of publicly favouring the transfer of the Chinese seat, and that if the invasion of South Korea had not been launched in June, France might well have come round in July or August, and been followed by Egypt or Ecuador, thus providing the seven votes needed for a breakthrough.†

Meanwhile Lie, seeing that the China deadlock would not be quickly broken, thought it his duty to keep the UN bridge between East and West from snapping altogether, and to get both sides to indicate on which points of conflict progress might be made – if not as things stood, then whenever negotiation became possible again.

In March he publicly called upon all governments to help shape a long-term programme 'to win peace through the United Nations'. He deliberately labelled it a 'twenty-year programme', to emphasize that he had no illusions about swift success. In April and May he visited Truman, Attlee, Bidault, and Stalin, presenting to each head of government a wide-ranging ten-point memorandum, and inviting their comments.

Such a spectacular initiative was certainly not in the minds of those who in 1945 had relegated the Secretary-General and his not too clearly defined functions to the tail end of the Charter. It might have been in Cecil's mind when he proposed a 'Chancellor' for the League; in Roosevelt's, when he (privately) threw off in 1942 the idea of naming the future UN's chief official the 'World's Moderator'; possibly in the minds of the State Department planners who, in early 1944, thought that the UN should have a political 'President' as well as an administrative

* 'He saw the hysteria invade high places and sweep his country in violation of fundamental principles of fair play and orderly justice by which he had lived all his life. The strain finally grew too strong, and he broke.' Trygve Lie, op. cit.

† Stephen M. Schwebel, *The Secretary-General of the United Nations*, page 147, Harvard University Press and Oxford University Press, 1952; and Lie, op. cit., pages 266–70.

Secretary-General.* But there was no such talk at San Francisco. Now, less than five years after San Francisco, not one government accused Lie of exceeding his powers. Most of them thanked him.

The content of his proposals aroused objections in both East and West, but no more than he had expected. The public argument about them (they were published on 6 June) was overlaid by the Korean war. When the Assembly debated his initiative in November, Korea had drawn the lines anew. He was commended in a fifty-one to five vote, after being savaged by Andrey Vishinsky ('The programme of the American monopolies is set forth in the memorandum') and by Malik, who alleged that

the fact that the memorandum was agreed on in advance with Washington arouses no doubt on anybody's part. The authors will not deny it.

Lie denied it, there and then, and effectively. He pointed out that he had drafted it in consultation only with his own staff, including, he made clear, his chief Soviet assistant, Constantin Zinchenko. He told Malik flatly that he must know he was lying. He might have added that in June the Soviet Press had honoured this programme, which Malik now spurned as 'permeated with servility towards America', by printing it in full. And that Stalin, when Lie visited the Kremlin in May, had told him that 'a mediator will always be criticized by both sides.... But you know, Mr Lie, the middle way in such situations will always win'. Stalin, Lie noted, smiled as he said this.

Whatever Stalin's smile meant, it vanished for ever on 25 June 1950. From that day on† Lie became, in Soviet

---

* Schwebel, op. cit., and Ruth B. Russell, *A History of the United Nations Charter*, Brookings Institution, Washington, 1958. British readers should be reminded that in North America the term 'president' often indicates a full-time chief executive, in business as well as in public institutions. A visa issued to one very modest friend of mine gives his occupation simply as 'president'; he is happily unaffected by this seeming grandeur.

† One week earlier Senator Knowland had asked the American government to try to oust the 'Soviet partisan' Lie.

official eyes, 'the abettor of American aggression' who, 'having discarded his mask, has given up all pretence of respecting the Charter'.

When Russia later vetoed his re-election, fought against the extension of his five-year term, and totally boycotted him from February 1951 on, it claimed that it was *not* punishing him for his part in activating the UN's effort to save South Korea. Instead, Vishinsky complained of his ten-point memorandum, and of his agreement to the creation of the 'illegal' UN commissions on Korea and the Balkans – that is, of things done long before the Korean war suddenly wiped off Stalin's smile. This was pure nonsense, the purpose of which may remain obscure until the Byzantine labyrinths of Kremlin politics are some day exposed to the historian's eyes. What Russia really could not forgive was that Trygve Lie had boldly done his duty when South Korea was invaded.

It is sometimes argued that Lie might have been spared the Soviet venom that eventually drove him from office, if he had played possum over Korea, doing only what he was specifically instructed to do and not a hand's turn more. Certainly, in terms of 'the Charter as it was meant to be',* a possum role would have been 'correct'. But after four years of bulldog tenacity in enlarging his active role, Lie could not be a Drummond now. The reports of the UN's own observers in Korea showed him that in this conflict mere resort to 'conciliation' would simply give the Communist invaders time to overrun the whole of the south (which they nearly did). America was obviously going to rush to South Korea's aid. Lie was determined that this first post-war response to cold-blooded invasion should be a UN response; to leave it all to America would be a denial of the whole purpose of the United Nations. He decided to come right out into the open.

---

* Lord Home's insistence (page 29) that the great powers should 'deal *together* with any breach of the peace by the smaller powers' meant tacit acceptance of the Soviet claim that the UN had no right to go to South Korea's rescue without Russia's consent.

Fast thinking was needed. At midnight, 24–5 June, he was telephoned at his suburban home in Forest Hills on Long Island by a State Department official, who passed on an urgent report that the North Korean army had struck south. He at once told Andrew Cordier, his American executive assistant, to ask for a special report from the UN observers in Korea, and 'Dragon' Protitch, a Yugoslav senior Security Council official, to prepare for an emergency meeting. He got little sleep that night. At 3 a.m. Gross made a formal American request for a Council meeting. Lie had the meeting fixed for 2 p.m. Before the Council assembled – at Lake Success, also on Long Island, where it and the Secretariat were then temporarily occupying part of a factory – Lie had talked with as many delegates as he could, chosen his own course, influenced some of theirs, and drafted (with Cordier and Feller) a statement which was to prove a turning-point in the history of his office.

Sir Benegal Rau of India, the Council president, gave him the floor first. Armed with the UN observers' new report, which had reached him at noon, Lie declared that the attack was a threat to international peace (he foresaw that Russia would label it a civil war), and that it was the Council's 'clear duty' to act to restore peace. He emphasized the Council's competence, thus rebutting in advance the Soviet argument that it was not competent because neither Moscow nor Peking was represented.

Lie continued to act vigorously both in pressing member states to contribute to the defence of South Korea, and in urging Washington to give full weight to the UN's role in what was physically an overwhelmingly American effort – although sixteen nations placed fighting forces under the Unified Command which the Council, on 7 July, requested the American government to organize in the name of the United Nations. He was active, too, in preparing for a settlement; notably, in canvassing a plan of his own at the end of September, by which time the original aggressors were in full retreat.

After the massive Chinese intervention, a mission from Peking led by General Wu came to UN headquarters for three weeks in December, nominally to complain about America's support of the Nationalists in Formosa, but showing itself also ready to discuss the Korean conflict. Oddly, while Wu urged a cease-fire, he would not meet the Assembly's cease-fire committee. This was the famous occasion when 'Rau did all the wooing, and Wu did all the rowing'. Still more oddly, the Peking man asked for the help of, and had nine private meetings – unproductive but civil – with, the Moscow-branded 'abettor of aggression', Trygve Lie.

Korea stimulated the growth of the UN 'as it was *not* meant to be' in several ways, all of them somewhat confusing or confused. The Council's call for aid for South Korea was possible only because Malik was not in his seat to veto it. As, 'next time', a Russian would doubtless be there to veto a similar call, the Assembly adopted in November the 'Uniting for Peace' resolution, with consequences only dimly seen at the time, if at all. The army that fought under the UN flag in Korea, mainly provided by one of the two super-powers, and grappling with an aggressor that was a creature of the other, was neither the kind of UN force that the Charter envisaged, nor the kind that later took shape in Sinai and the Congo. Yet it was still an international force, sponsored by the UN if not directed by it, and its long travail was an undoubted part of the birth-pangs of a new sense of collective responsibility for peace-keeping.

Lie afterwards said that he had exercised on 25 June his right under Article 99 of the Charter, which provides that

the Secretary-General may bring to the attention of the Security Council any matter which in his opinion may threaten the maintenance of international peace and security.

Strictly, he had not; at least, not alone, for America had already requested an urgent Council meeting. But his bold snatching up of the initiative clearly set a great precedent.

Only once – on 13 July 1960 – has Article 99 been specifically invoked; Hammarskjöld used it to summon the Council that day and set in train the massive UN Congo operation. But both Lie and Hammarskjöld repeatedly wielded it as a sheathed weapon, stimulating member governments to action (or to better behaviour) by privately saying that they were thinking of using it, and citing it to establish their right to do things which it implicitly necessitates, such as sending missions to get the facts on which a decision whether or not to invoke the article can be based (see pages 89 and 116). Korea at least sharpened it in the sheath.

Finally, Korea set off the three-year Soviet vendetta against Lie, the struggle over the Assembly's extension of his term after Russia had vetoed his re-election, and his eventual resignation after enduring two years of boycott broken only by vituperation. If this showed that a veto-wielding great power could, in the end, oust a Secretary-General who offended it, it also showed that the ousting would not always prove easy, quick, or cheap. Russia did not win friends or influence people, except against itself, by its vendetta. Not one government lined up with the Soviet bloc when the 1950 Assembly voted, forty-six to five, to extend Lie's term. Even Nationalist China, which had earlier threatened to veto him itself, and the Arabs, bitter as they were over Palestine, merely abstained.

This was the background against which Hammarskjöld took office in April 1953.

Dag Hammarskjöld, then forty-seven, was first suggested for the post by France, which secured Soviet agreement before taking the candidature any further; the irony of this origin, in the light of later events, is telling. The Council's unanimous nomination surprised both the world at large, which had never seen his name listed among the 'possibles' (or, indeed, anywhere else), and the man himself. He had been leading Sweden's Assembly delegation in New York only a few weeks earlier, and had heard no whisper of his name being discussed; when the first word reached him on the eve of April Fool's Day, he took it for a hoax. But there was logic in this improbability, though it proved a mistaken logic.

Although he had been deputy foreign minister since 1951, Hammarskjöld had never belonged to a party or even campaigned for election. A self-styled 'technician', he had a brilliant reputation among professionals as an administrator and government economist: official chief of the finance ministry at thirty, chairman of the Riksbank at thirty-six, he came into international economics in 1947 as a delegate to O.E.E.C. meetings, and thence moved to the foreign ministry, still primarily as an economist. As a discreet back-room type, skilled in conciliation, adept at not giving offence, he appealed to the French and British, who had not liked Lie's break with the Drummond tradition; he was acceptable to Russia; few Americans knew him, and some wondered if he was not a bit too prudent for the job, but Secretary of State Dulles was persuaded within a week to approve a man he had never heard of before.

Naturally, Hammarskjöld was measured against the fellow Scandinavian who had preceded him; and the glaring contrasts blinded many people to some basic similarities. Where Lie was irked by complexities, and at times ended by trying to thrust through them, bull-headed, Hammarskjöld actually relished any challenge to his unusual powers of analysis and dissection. Lie yearned for the blunt honesties of his homeland; Hammarskjöld's literary ear was always cocked for nice diplomatic nuances. Lie, an old hand on the hustings, liked to touch a chord of simple appeal; Hammarskjöld's statements were fine-spun webs of unassailable, but sometimes almost intolerable, reasoning. Lie was a homely man, eager for friendliness and ill at ease in state, rather lost in New York, happy if he could share decisions with his family circle; Hammarskjöld, though drawing strongly on the background of his own remarkable family, moved everywhere with the lonely and self-sufficient poise of a true mandarin. Traversing the long corridor that links the Secretariat tower with the Assembly hall, Lie's burly mass sometimes betrayed a touch of anxiety about whom he was likely to meet. Hammarskjöld would tread the same thick carpet delicately, a cat who walked by himself, tidily avoiding every eye he did not wish to catch. In their critics' view, the first was too human, the second not human enough.

But the belief that Hammarskjöld was 'safe' in contrast to the 'over-energetic' Lie, that he would be content with a non-political role, or would at least do his politicking only in the decent obscurity of the back room, was to prove just one more of those UN illusions.

Hammarskjöld has often been branded as 'subtle' – a damning brand, at least among the British, who, as others are often astonished to find, regard bluff simplicity as one of their own national virtues. Subtler than Lie, in style and method, he clearly was; but behind the master craftsman's skill, the sometimes convoluted philosophy which he developed for the UN, there lay an essential straightforwardness. It was partly this quality that enabled him to keep, or regain, surprisingly widespread confidence even when he had got into exposed and vulnerable positions.

Lie, at the end of his service, had bluntly told the Assembly that

to strengthen, for the critical times ahead, the office of the Secretary-General in the framework of the United Nations and to enhance its influence for peace in the world ... has always been my first consideration. ...

Looking back after his resignation, he also wrote:

My eyes were wide open as I pushed my way into each of the many problems that arose. ... The Secretary-General is obligated to risk himself. ... I felt morally and legally compelled to take what I saw as the 'United Nations view', particularly when I felt that the member states were not living up to their Charter obligations.*

* Lie, op. cit.

Hammarskjöld's finer-woven web was of the same pattern. Characteristically, he was in no hurry to declare his intentions, and when he did, it was in words that were anything but blunt – though their purport was clear. Only when he was being re-elected for a second five-year term did he first spell out, in a speech to the Assembly on 26 September 1957, his main principle of action. (Again characteristically, he began it with a negative statement.)

I do not believe that the Secretary-General should be *asked* to act, by the member states, if no guidance for his action is to be found either in the Charter or in the decisions of the main organs of the UN. Within the limits thus set, however, I believe it to be his duty to use his office, and indeed the machinery of the Organization, *to its utmost capacity.* . . .

. . . . The Secretary-General should be *expected* to act also *without* such guidance, should this appear *to him* necessary in order to help in *filling any vacuum* that may appear in the systems which the Charter and traditional diplomacy provide for the safeguarding of peace and security. [Author's italics.]

By May 1959 he was publicly claiming – in a speech on the eve of the four-power Geneva conference on Germany – the right to 'express what may be called the independent judgement of the Organization'. By October he was arguing, in a TV interview, that the limitations of the Assembly and Council in handling dangerous situations made it necessary 'to create a new executive responsibility somewhere'; and that 'it is on the basis of this inter-pretation that quite a few recent developments have taken place, also on my own initiative'.

But there was a long quiet phase before Hammarskjöld set out on this road. Those who thought him a 'safer' man than Lie were encouraged by the record of his first two years, when he occupied himself very largely with ad-ministration. The circumstances, however, were mis-leading. The whole UN was then having a pretty quiet time. Korea got its armistice in 1953, and the member states licked their wounds. The 1954 crisis and settlement in Indo-China were kept well away from the UN. The struggle over the European Defence Community, and the struggle for the succession in Russia, held the attention of the powers. 'Summitry' was in the air; the UN was half forgotten.

Hammarskjöld was able to work himself into his job without having to face immediate crises, a privilege denied to Lie – and to be denied to U Thant. Although Lie's ultimate fate was presented to Hammarskjöld as a warning, Lie had won the essential battles of procedure, and his successor had no need to fight for the right to speak his mind.

When the first call to action – public, personal action – came, at the end of 1954, he was ready; ready and, some thought, only too willing.

Communist China had revealed that it still held eleven American airmen, who had been missing since their aircraft was shot down in Korea twenty months earlier, and that they had been given long prison sentences. Angered Americans demanded a blockade of the China coast. Eisenhower and Dulles preferred to take the case to the UN Assembly, which asked Hammarskjöld to seek the release of the prisoners 'by the means most appropriate in his judgement'.

This was the first, in a sense the classic, case of 'leaving it to Dag'. The Assembly gave him this first of a succession of 'use your own judgement' mandates because it had no idea what could be done. Hammarskjöld did have an idea. Before the Assembly voted, he told his close friend, Hans Engen, Norway's UN representative, that he would try to go to Peking himself. He foresaw the dangers. His decision to go at once brought angry cries of 'suppliant' from right-wing Americans, then spoiling for a showdown with China. He could not be sure that Peking would respond to his request for an invitation at all. And if he got there, but achieved nothing, his office and the UN as a whole would lose an incalculable amount of 'face'.

Chou En-lai came through with the invitation – accepting without comment Hammarskjöld's inclusion in his party of an American, his personal aide and bodyguard, William Ranallo.* In January 1955, in a bitterly cold Peking, the Secretary-General had four days of formal and extremely elliptical discussion with Chou, whose subtle diplomatic style, he said later, made him feel a barbarian. There was, however, a certain meeting of minds between the two mandarins, though they were never to meet again.

Hammarskjöld returned to New York refusing to say in public anything more definite than that 'the door that has been opened can be kept open, given restraint on all sides'. Privately, he told the American UN representative, Henry Cabot Lodge, that he was now confident the airmen would be freed, but not until China could free them without seeming to yield to pressure. In the next few months tension in the Formosa straits first mounted and then waned. Eisenhower and Dulles reined in some of the more hot-headed 'China lobby' Americans. India pressed Peking to free the airmen; Hammarskjöld kept on discreetly prodding, and used a trip to Sweden at the end of April to nudge the Chinese ambassador there. In August the airmen were released. Hammarskjöld, who, Lodge had said, had 'put his life's reputation as a diplomat on the chopping block' by deciding to go to Peking, had got it off again.

His next 'use your own judgement' mandate came from the Council, which in April 1956 asked him to 'survey' the increasingly violated armistice agreements between Israel and its Arab enemies, and to arrange 'any measures' that would reduce tension.

The UN Truce Supervision Organization (UNTSO), set up after Ralph Bunche's Nobel-winning feat in securing the Palestine armistices in 1949, was then struggling, with its staff of 120 led by the patient, taciturn Canadian General Burns, against a rising tide of raids and reprisals, ominously backed by a new arms race set off by Soviet deliveries of tanks, aircraft, and guns to Egypt. Hammar-

* Ranallo (formerly aide to Lie too) served Hammarskjöld to the end, and was killed with him in September 1961.

skjöld spent a month in shuttling briskly between the antagonists' five capitals, accompanied by Burns and by George Ivan Smith of the Secretariat, who acted as spokesman, in so far as there was anything that could be said without upsetting some applecart; there generally was not. Ivan Smith's forced reliance, under a rain of Press inquiries, on two good non-committal adjectives to describe the evolving situation, soon led him and Hammarskjöld to address each other as Mr Flexible and Mr Fluid.

Mr Flexible got back to New York in May with a set of fresh assurances from the Arab and Israel governments that they would reciprocally observe the cease-fire provision in the armistice terms. The worsening trend seemed checked for a moment. 'Incidents' and violent talk fell off. But the Council, meeting in June, contributed only another joust between Russia and the West. And in July came the Egyptian nationalizing of the Suez Canal.

By early October the canal dispute had been brought to the Council by Britain and France. Hammarskjöld contrived the cutting short of public debate as quickly as possible. He got the British, French, and Egyptian foreign ministers – Selwyn Lloyd, Christian Pineau, Mahmoud Fawzi – into his own office up on the thirty-eighth floor. There, in half a dozen informal sessions round a small coffee table, they agreed on six principles: freedom of passage; respect for Egypt's sovereignty; insulation of the canal operation from all domestic politics; the levying of tolls to be agreed between Egypt and the users; part of the tolls to go to canal development; arbitration of unresolved issues between Egypt and the dispossessed canal company. The Council unanimously approved these six points, when Britain and France presented them; but Dmitri Shepilov, then Soviet foreign minister, vetoed the rest of the Franco–British draft resolution, which, while commending the eighteen 'user' countries' plan for international canal management, asked Egypt to offer alternative proposals that conformed to the six points.

Hammarskjöld was not dismayed by this veto. He got – or so he thought – the agreement of Lloyd, Pineau, and Fawzi to resume meeting privately, with Hammarskjöld again playing chaperon (as he put it), in Geneva – on 29 October.

But 29 October had a different dawn. Israel invaded Sinai.

On 30 October Britain and France vetoed the American cease-fire resolution in the Council, after themselves sending an ultimatum to Egypt (and, irrelevantly, to Israel) demanding that their own forces should take over the canal.

Hammarskjöld was shaken to the core. Britain and France were the two major powers to which his European background had related him most closely. Their action forced him to reconsider his whole relationship with the great-power Council members. A showdown between the UN and Russia was already looming up; an emergency Council meeting on 27 October had produced bitter exchanges about the fighting in Hungary, though between 28 October and 2 November the Soviet Army seemed to be pulling out. On 31 October Hammarskjöld addressed the Council in terms that were widely misinterpreted as a threat to resign. In fact he had no intention of resigning. His speech served notice that, whatever the powers chose to do, the Secretary-General must serve the Charter: '... its aims must ultimately determine what for him is right and wrong. For that he must stand'. He repeated this warning in the context of Hungary on 4 November.

The Suez–Sinai conflict transformed the UN. It brought alive the 'Uniting for Peace' resolution of 1950, hitherto never applied. On 1 November the Assembly began its first emergency session – an all-night one. Lester Pearson, Canada's foreign minister, at once began to canvass privately his plan for an international UN force – to be provided, unprecedentedly, by the smaller states – that could disentangle the belligerents ('We have to get them off the hook,' he told Engen) and thereafter stabilize the danger area. Before dawn on 2 November he publicly broached the idea to the Assembly. Over lunch that day he convinced an at first dubious Hammarskjöld.

At 2 a.m. on 4 November the Assembly, on 'Mike' Pearson's motion, asked the Secretary-General to produce a plan for a UN force within forty-eight hours. At midnight, on Engen's motion, it approved his first outline, including the appointment of Burns as commander. On 7 November it approved his fuller plan, asked him and Burns to organize the force, and voted him wide authority to 'take all other necessary administrative and executive actions'.

All this was thrust upon Hammarskjöld, not initiated by him. But the UN emergency force (UNEF) could not have been conjured up to play its crucial role if he and his staff had not flung themselves into its creation as soon as Pearson's project found acceptance. They tackled the problem of clearing the now blocked canal with the same furious energy. And within a matter of days Hammarskjöld found himself necessarily acting in the diplomatic even more than the administrative field. He and Burns and Cordier had to work hard on President Nasser to get agreement about the terms on which the force would enter Egypt – where it was at first suspected (not unnaturally in view of what Britain and France were saying) of being a device to impose international control of the canal. They could not get Israel's agreement for UNEF to operate on its side of the border at all. But in the following months Hammarskjöld was continuously involved in the process of getting Israel to complete its withdrawal.

Most of this was behind-the-scenes work, so discreetly executed that he was accused of cold-shouldering the Israelis when he was in daily contact with them. Only the top of the massive iceberg of his diplomacy was visible, in the convoluted form of his 'reports' to the impatient Assembly. In these he delivered guarded but significant warnings to all parties, as well as indicating the courses he was setting as the situation evolved, and appealing for support.*

At this stage he began to use the technique of publicly presenting an 'interpretation' of, or an 'assumption' about, the terms of resolutions (or of the Charter), and waiting to see if it was challenged. If it was not, he could later cite the point (sometimes in a quite different context) as having been tacitly accepted. He was thus to develop a remarkable set of precedents.

His careful wording aggrieved newspapermen, who found it impossible to summarize statements that were as cunningly balanced as any mobile, and annoyed some of the ministers and diplomats with whom he had to deal. Selwyn Lloyd awarded him 'first prize for ambiguity'. Others, however, praised his 'calculated imprecisions'. They were always calculated; they left room for manoeuvre, concealed temporary deadlocks, and saved face all round – including that of some who complained of his vagueness. Hammarskjöld believed in the formula sometimes used to define a gentleman: one who is rude only when he means to be. If he could, he would always get a point across in language that would not force the person addressed to take umbrage. Politicians, it must be noted, often have to take umbrage, not because they are actually angry, but from fear that domestic critics will accuse them of failing to stand up for their country.

By April 1957 Israel's forces were all back in Israel, and the Suez Canal cleared; ships were moving freely up the

---

* A vivid recollection from this period is of arriving in New York in February 1957, when the Assembly was close to calling for economic sanctions against Israel because it had not given up the Gaza area, and reading two headlines: 'Dag For Sanctions', and 'Dag Slams Sanctions'. Both purported to describe his latest report. As this suggested that the document must be even harder to construe than usual, it seemed a good idea to ask one of his close associates about it before getting down to reading it. This man turned out to have been up most of the night helping Hammarskjöld draft the report. What did it really say to the Assembly? His reply: 'It says: "Think".'

long-blockaded Gulf of Aqaba to Israel's southern port at Eilat; one more dash by Hammarskjöld to Cairo had defused tension over Egyptian re-entry into Gaza; and the UN force stood guard along the restored frontier, blocking the guerrilla raids that had formerly enraged the Israelis. Hammarskjöld's stock stood high: most particularly in America and among the Afro-Asians; but, characteristically, he was eager to mend all his fences, and he made a point of visiting Britain and France as soon as he could.

In September came his unanimous re-election for a second five-year term, to start in April 1958; of this he was fated to serve only three and a half years, and they were to be crowded. At his re-election, he declared the doctrine of 'filling vacuums' (quoted on page 101); and in November 1957 he embarked on a little-remembered but significant personal venture.

An obscure running quarrel between Israel and Jordan about Israeli access to the enclave of Mount Scopus, north-east of Jerusalem, had worsened to the point of Jordan declaring that it no longer had any confidence in Colonel Leary, the American acting head of UNTSO since Burns's move to UNEF. Hammarskjöld flew to Jerusalem and managed to plug this ugly little 'vacuum'. He said a little later, in private, that this time he felt he was out entirely on his own, and 'I simply had to succeed'.

In July 1958 it was noticed that the Secretary-General who had often advocated 'quiet diplomacy' was being unprecedentedly vocal in the Council's public debates on Lebanon. On 22 July he filled his first big vacuum.

To help America extricate the troops it had landed in Lebanon, in response to President Chamoun's urgent appeal, a week earlier, Japan had proposed that the Council empower Hammarskjöld to 'take such measures . . . as he may consider necessary' – meaning, mainly, that he could enlarge the hundred-man UN observer group in Lebanon (UNOGIL) which had been set up in June. Russia vetoed this resolution, on the ground that it did not specifically demand immediate American withdrawal.

(Having the embarrassed Americans on a hook, Russia had little reason to help them get off gracefully.)

Hammarskjöld promptly announced that he would do what the veto prevented the Council from authorizing: enlarge UNOGIL. (He built it up to a much more effective size, 500 strong at its peak.) He cited both his September 1957 statement on 'filling vacuums', and his statement of 31 October 1956 (page 105). This time he was not flatly defying Russia, which had already indicated readiness to see UNOGIL enlarged; in fact, he was more conspicuously at odds with his native Sweden, which had reacted to the American landing by demanding that the UN observers be pulled out. In these circumstances, he achieved a further extension of his own authority without opposition.

When the Lebanon–Jordan crisis was switched to an emergency Assembly session in August, the newly articulate Hammarskjöld jumped in in the first half-hour to offer a wide-ranging programme, whose key provisions were: UNOGIL to be replaced, when the time was ripe, by some other 'form of UN representation' in Lebanon; 'special measures ... adequate in the specific situation prevailing in Jordan'; and the reaffirming by all Arab states of the pledges of mutual respect they had given each other in the Arab League charter.

This emergency Assembly was a much flatter affair than the Suez sessions. The worst of the crisis was in fact over before it met; the problem was one of disengagement. The flatness actually drove Hammarskjöld to come out into the open himself with his plan; there was no panic, and no Pearson. Hans Engen, however, volunteered to lead the 'fire brigade', and exhausted himself canvassing a resolution which, in essence, proposed 'leaving it to Dag'. Perhaps because Engen was too warmly embraced by the Americans and British, he could not find Afro-Asian backers. Perhaps it was because the Arabs were coming round to Hammarskjöld's idea that self-respect required them to handle a primarily inter-Arab problem themselves. After two oddly desultory weeks, all eleven Arab governments got together and quickly agreed, in a state of almost startling euphoria, a joint resolution that looked even more like Hammarskjöld's initial programme than Engen's had done – and gave him yet another 'use your own judgement' mandate to make

such practical arrangements as would adequately help in upholding the purposes and principles of the Charter in relation to Lebanon and Jordan in the present circumstances, and thereby to facilitate the early withdrawal of the foreign troops. ...

Everybody sounded happy – even Hammarskjöld, who, many feared, had really laid his neck on the chopping block this time. Lebanon was going to be all right, but, despite the new inter-Arab 'good neighbour' pledges, nobody expected King Hussein's Jordan to stay on the map once the British troops pulled out.

Jordan was still there in 1963, the British having left in November 1958. Nobody was quite sure why; but Hammarskjöld's three weeks of very quiet diplomacy indeed in Amman, Cairo, and other capitals after the emergency Assembly had something to do with it. His only tangible creation was a UN office in Jordan – a 'presence' with a staff of thirty headed by Pier Spinelli, the Italian director of the UN's European office in Geneva. Yet this modest installation served two very necessary purposes. At critical moments – as when, in November, the aircraft carrying Hussein to Europe was nearly shot down by Syrian MiGs – the UN presence had a steadying effect; and its continuous, impartial reporting to Hammarskjöld offset the flood of wild distortions and exaggerations that the Arab tensions still produced.

Hammarskjöld also proposed to appoint a 'high-level' representative at UN headquarters who could visit the various Arab countries as required for 'diplomatic actions'. But this official (at once nicknamed 'the absent presence') was never appointed; the Secretary-General found things going smoothly enough to dispense with the idea. During 1959 Spinelli was already able to divide his time between

Amman and Geneva. Early in 1960 he began to visit Jordan only very occasionally.

The Spinelli mission had, however, made quiet history. It introduced the world to the phrase 'a UN presence', which soon acquired an almost mystic* quality. And it was a semi-permanent UN 'subsidiary body' that had been created by the Secretary-General, on the strength of his vague mandate to make 'practical arrangements'. The precedents were piling up.

So were the risks. A perceptive commentary by one of the shrewdest newspapermen at UN headquarters† pointed out that his record since Suez already indicated that 'he thrives on crises'; that these crises had led to a quite unexpected enlargement of his powers; but that he was 'living more dangerously, now that he has embarked on the course of increasingly "writing his own ticket".'

'Living dangerously' did not mean acting spectacularly. In fact, the deepest irony of Hammarskjöld's situation was that he was most vulnerable to charges of exceeding his powers when he chose a method that kept things quiet. If, on the other hand, he dodged responsibility and referred a problem to Council or Assembly, demanding a definite mandate before he would act, there was liable to be a public slambang in debate that might well make matters worse.

In December 1958 he chose the perils of quietness, and got away with it so completely that there is hardly a trace in the world's memory of his feat. Such is the penalty of success in peacemaking.

Suspicion had been building up between neutralist Cambodia and Western-allied Thailand (Siam). Cambodian anger was, at least symbolically, centred on the Thais'

---

* After Jordan had told the emergency Assembly that it wanted no 'substantial' UN presence, much talk (in the delegates' bar, if not in more sober quarters) turned on suitable names for an insubstantial presence. After UNTSO, UNEF, and UNOGIL, one favoured term was UNICORN – a suitably mystical and elusive beast to join with the British lion in the struggle around the Jordanian crown.

† Sven Ahman, 'Mr Hammarskjöld's Not-So-Quiet Diplomacy', in the *Reporter* of 4 September 1958.

seizure of the ancient Buddhist temple of Preah Vihear, or Phra Vihar, which lies in such tangled border mountains that it is virtually inaccessible. Other less romantic but perhaps graver issues, involving relations with Peking, fed the fire. After frontier clashes, street demonstrations, and abusive radio and Press exchanges, diplomatic relations were broken off, Cambodian police seized a number of Thais near the border, and Thailand closed the frontier altogether. Both governments sent formal accusations to the UN.

Hammarskjöld foresaw that, if he operated 'the Charter as it was meant to be' and laid the charges before the Council, the great-power members would get into a public row about the respective perils of Communism and of Western alliances, which would make the local crisis harder to resolve. He kept the case out of the Council altogether (but privately consulted its members).

He secured from Sweden the services of an able retired diplomat, Baron Johan Beck-Friis, and sent him as his own special representative to 'help the two governments find a path towards better relations'. By February 1959 all the Thais in Cambodian hands had been freed, diplomatic relations were restored, and the frontier reopened. The temple dispute was in due course taken to the International Court at The Hague (whose eventual verdict in favour of Cambodia, in 1962, was to set off a fresh outburst of indignation in Thailand).

At subsequent Press conferences, Hammarskjöld played the thing down; 'a fairly simple case', he said, which could well have gone to the Council and ended much the same way. However, the parties involved had preferred to ask him to 'send someone to assist them', which he had done 'without in any way making this a precedent'. This last phrase evoked some gently sceptical smiles, which broadened when he added:

You can see how much more effective and smooth-working such a technique is than the regular one, which involves all the meetings and debates and so on.

In the introduction to his 1959 annual report, he continued the codifying of his new methods. The working methods indicated in the Charter, he argued, might be 'supplemented by others, under the pressure of circumstances'; the new ones could become a kind of 'common law'. His own initiatives were 'in strict accordance with the Charter', within the competence of his office, and, moreover, he had always kept the members of 'the appropriate organs of the UN' informed.

Back-stage tasks tended to evolve, now that the way had been cleared by precedent, into rather more active but still discreet operations. Late in 1959 Hammarskjöld himself was engaged in quiet talks with British and Saudi Arabian representatives about their long-standing disputes, particularly the one over the Buraimi oasis area. This led to his dispatch in 1960 of another quiet Swedish diplomat, Herbert de Ribbing (Ambassador in Madrid), to the areas and capital concerned with the Buraimi affair, to examine the problem and report.

But things could not always be kept so quiet. The course of events in Laos in 1959 led Hammarskjöld to take personal action there in public defiance of Russia, and in the face of some sharp American criticism too.

Prince Souvanna Phouma's attempt to hold together a coalition government including pro-Communist Laotians had broken down in 1958; and the American-backed right-wing government that then took office, failing to suppress the pro-Communist armed forces that still controlled areas near the North Vietnam border, began in 1959 to complain to the UN that Communist North Vietnam was intervening in support of these forces. By August the government was asking for UN observers to be sent. This request had American backing; but Hammarskjöld's response was cautious. He told a Press conference that

if it were a case of one of these fairly new-fangled initiatives of the Secretary-General acting without authorization or without a formal decision of any of the other organs, he can never permit himself to act, so to say, in a legally ambiguous way.

One of the legal issues he had in mind was the argument, pressed by Russia, that the Laos situation required not UN action but the reactivating of the international machinery set up by the 1954 Geneva agreements on Indo-China. Another was the distinction between a border conflict and a problem affecting only one country. Summarizing the precedents, in a statement issued on 27 August, he argued that he himself could send a fact-finding representative if the terms of reference were purely Laotian; but that a mission concerning the border would require either an invitation from both countries involved (as in the Cambodia–Thailand case) or an Assembly or Council decision.

On 4 September the Laotian government, alarmed by fresh border attacks, appealed for a UN emergency force to be sent 'to halt aggression'. Hammarskjöld, cutting short a tour in Latin-America, flew back to New York, where the Council met on 7 September. He made it clear that he was not invoking Article 99. Nor did he endorse Laos's assertion that aggression was being committed. (Lodge did, in the name of the American government.) At 1 a.m. next morning the Council voted, ten to one, to set up an investigating sub-committee of four of its members (Argentina, Italy, Japan, Tunisia).

Russia's veto was overruled by the Council chairman, Egidio Ortona of Italy, on the ground that the decision was a procedural one. Arkady Sobolev – a former Assistant Secretary-General, who by now was chief Soviet representative at the UN – declared this to be illegal; but Ortona's ruling was upheld by another ten-to-one vote. The sub-committee spent four weeks in Laos, and reported in early November that North Vietnam had been helping the Laotian rebels but had not, on the evidence, sent its own troops across the border.

Here was another 'vacuum'. Russia would obviously veto any move in the Council for further UN action. (Even among American lawyers there was doubt about the overruling of 7 September; and the sub-committee's revelation that Laos's charges had been exaggerated might make it difficult to muster as solid a front against Russia a second time.) Moreover, Hammarskjöld saw little hope of easing Laos's plight by tactics that brought the great powers into direct collision. He decided he must act independently, courting certain Soviet and probable American displeasure, but calculating that both powers would in the end be glad to be helped off the Laotian hook.

He told the Council members that he would go to Laos himself, and would install there a representative to report to him on future developments. Sobolev protested that this 'can only further complicate the situation', and the Soviet Press used still sharper language. Hammarskjöld went, just the same. While in Laos he summoned Sakari Tuomioja, the Finnish banker, diplomat, and ex-premier who was then in charge of the UN Economic Commission for Europe. Tuomioja remained in Laos until January 1960, and was followed there by Roberto Heurtematte, a senior UN economic official from Panama, and, in February, by Dr Edouard Zellweger, who was posted to Laos indefinitely as 'Special Consultant to the Secretary-General'.

None of this was an overtly political 'presence'. Hammarskjöld described the work of his representatives as purely concerned with promoting Laos's economic growth and stability. But Zellweger's background as a distinguished Swiss jurist and diplomat was noted, not unfairly, as evidence that he was acting as a political representative too. Also noted (when it leaked out) was a significant message that Hammarskjöld sent to the King of Laos in January 1960, just after General Phoumi Nosavan had seized power there, expressing hope that the country's basic policies – including its neutrality – were not going to be changed. There is no doubt that he used all his influence to try to get Laos back on to the path of neutralism and national reconciliation; that he was disturbed by the way the American-backed right wing once again precipitated conflict in 1960, and pleased when, in early 1961, the new Kennedy government accepted a neutral Laos as the right objective.

The Russians never had any illusions about the UN 'presence' in Laos being purely economic. But Hammarskjöld's calculation proved correct. After their initial protests in November 1959 they fell silent.

Late in 1960, however, after Khrushchev had launched his campaign against the Secretary-General – both the man and the office – Soviet delegates in the Assembly criticized the Laos action in stronger terms than they had used at the time it was taken. But their belated charges that Hammarskjöld had 'exceeded his competence' merely gave him an opportunity to state his case for acting. He stated it effectively. His defence of his own journey to Laos was an echo of Trygve Lie's argument in September 1946 (page 89):

If the Secretary-General is entitled to draw the attention of the Security Council to threats to peace and security, has he to rely on reports in the Press or from this or that government? Has he to take the word of Moscow or Washington? No, certainly not. He has to find out for himself, and that may mean, as in the case of the criticized journey to Laos last November, that he has to go himself. To deny the Secretary-General the right to such personal fact-finding is, in fact, to erase from the Charter Article 99.

In defending the establishment of the UN mission in Laos, he openly appealed for the support of the whole body of small 'new nations':

Those countries who wish to have the independent assistance of the United Nations, in the modest forms possible for the Secretary-General, and without running into the stormy weather of a major international political debate, will certainly be interested in the attitude of the delegate of the Soviet Union.

His action in Laos embodied the main elements in his now strongly developing idea that the main concern of the UN should be with the fate of the small and weak nations.

The events of 1956 had forced him to rethink the whole question of the great powers' role in the UN. From then on, in place of the 1945 concept of them jointly acting as world policemen, there evolved the idea that in most cases of local conflict it was important to keep them out; or, if they had already got embrangled, to get them out. Troubles in, or between, weak 'new nations' were liable to draw the powers in unless a UN presence of some kind could be installed to steady things and discourage open intervention. UN economic aid could both be a tactful cover for a political presence, and have a steadying effect in itself.

Hammarskjöld thought that the powers might often, in the end, be relieved if UN action saved them from being sucked into a risky and doubtfully profitable struggle. But he foresaw that they would not always be able to consent to such action publicly. Hence the value of establishing his right to act (as in Laos) without a mandate at all, and even in the face of a great power's formal disapproval. Hence, also, the importance of identifying his office as far as possible with the general will of the smaller states.

In 1959 he was already publicly asserting that it was his right to take up an independent position on any particular issue, basing himself on 'United Nations opinion' – the opinion of the mass of nations not directly partisan to that dispute.* In regard to disarmament, he said, the UN's role *vis-à-vis* the powers was that of 'an element representing all the rest of the world'.†

He spelt things out extensively in the introduction to his 1960 annual report:

There are in the Charter elements of a thinking which, I believe, belongs to an earlier period in the development of the world community. I have in mind, especially, the concept that the permanent members of the Security Council should not only, as is natural, be recognized as carrying special responsibility for peace and security, but that, further, these permanent members, working together, should represent a kind of 'built-in' directing group for the world community as organized in the United Nations. The fifteen years which have passed since the founding of the UN have witnessed a different development. . . .

So much for getting 'back to working the Charter as it

* Speech at Copenhagen, 2 May.
† Television interview, 16 October.

was meant to be'. With typical understatement, Hammarskjöld commented on the fact that the UN had provided its members not only with a conference machinery but also with 'an effective executive organ for joint action':

> The evolution has taken a course somewhat different from the one envisaged at San Francisco, but ... the departure as to methods is not considerable, and the conformity as to aims is complete.

He emphasized – with reference to the Middle East and Laos as well as the Congo, where the storm had broken by the time he was writing this report – that, where conflict arose as a 'result of ... a power vacuum between the two main blocs', the UN's 'preventive action must ... aim at filling the vacuum so that it will not provoke action from any of the major parties' which 'might in turn lead to counter-action from the other side'. In emerging Africa, in particular, the UN must do all it could to help the Africans to 'choose their own way'.

This was the basis of his lightning-swift response to the Congo government's appeal for UN military aid in July 1960. When the appeal arrived, on 12 July, he had already dashed back to New York from Geneva on hearing of the army mutiny and the flying in of Belgian troops; Ralph Bunche was already in Leopoldville; and they were already asking African member governments about what help they could give, through the UN, to reorganize and retrain the Congolese soldiery. On 13 July Hammarskjöld urgently summoned the Council himself under Article 99. In a seven-hour meeting that ended at 3.30 a.m., he and Mongi Slim of Tunisia, the only African on the Council, pushed through the resolution that authorized the creation of the UN Congo force. France at one point looked like vetoing it, but in the end abstained, as did Britain and Nationalist China. Russia did not like it, and sought delay, but yielded to strong pressure from the Africans – after accusing Bunche of plotting for American intervention. Hammarskjöld emphasized that this should be a primarily African operation. He had already asked Morocco,

Tunisia, Ghana, and Ethiopia for troops; and within four days 3,500 soldiers from those four countries had been flown in, mainly by American aircraft.

The Congo demanded a far more complex UN role than that played by the force on the Egypt–Israel border. Those of its complexities that led to the 1961 fighting in the Katanga are described in the next chapter. The whole story, in part familiar, in part unrevealed – and unfinished – cannot be set out here. Its real impact on the evolving character of the UN executive may be understood only when the story is fully ended and fully known.

Like Lie just ten years earlier, Hammarskjöld found himself violently denounced and eventually boycotted by Russia. But, unlike Lie, he was not being opposed by only one angry great power. Although the Soviet attack was unmatched in its virulence and openness, he encountered opposition from each of the other major powers as well at one stage or another in the Congo operation. Required to work within the limits set by a consensus that was achieved only with difficulty, he repeatedly found that consensus falling apart behind him. Fierce divisions appeared at times even among the African and Asian states to whom the success of the Congo operation was an evident and vital necessity.

In his 1961 annual report, published three weeks before his death, he wrote of the UN's 'thankless and easily misunderstood role' in the Congo, where it

had to pursue a line which, by safeguarding the free choice of the people, implied resistance against all efforts from outside to influence the outcome. In doing so, the Organization has been put in a position in which those within the country who felt disappointed in not getting its support ... accused the Organization of partiality, and in which, further, such outside elements as tried to get or protect a foothold within the country, when meeting an obstacle in the UN, made similar accusations.

A shrewd comment on the nature of much Western criticism of the Congo operation has been made by H. G. Nicholas in an article in *Encounter* (February 1962):

The issue is repeatedly presented in terms of an impossible
'either – or' – of an ideally enlightened, evolutionary and
pacific policy, such as a colonialist power operating the most
altruistic form of trusteeship might conceivably aspire to ...
versus a muddled, incompetent, ill informed, inexperienced,
partisan and polyglot UN operation. ... The real alternatives ...
are quite simply either a UN-sponsored policy, necessarily largely
Afro-Asian manned, and openly aimed at fostering African
nationalism and independence, or else a free-for-all with an
absolute certainty of Soviet intrusion on a massive scale and a
near certainty of conflict quickly developing from civil strife to
inter-African war and finally to inter-continental war.

Both physically and politically, the developing role of
the UN's unforeseen executive has been pressed hard
against its present upper limits throughout the operation
in the Congo. Again and again it has been said that the
UN has got in 'beyond its depth'; and at times it has
indeed been difficult to see how the organization could
stand the growing strain, let alone achieve any final solution.
Yet its record in the Congo suggests that there is some
truth in the argument that it thrives on crises, that its mus-
cles are most likely to develop when under strain.

There can certainly be no doubting that it has shown an
unexpected capacity for overcoming the blocking moves
made from various quarters; unexpected and, to some,
unwelcome. Khrushchev was visibly frustrated by the
non-aligned countries' rejection in 1960, and again in
1961, of his 'troika' plan (pages 39–42) for the hamstringing of the Secretariat. The prospect of financial
strangulation, as a result of the withholding of funds for the
UN's new operational costs by France and other Western
countries as well as by the Soviet bloc, was at least temporarily averted by U Thant's initiative in selling bonds
to member governments. There is every indication that
the UN executive will continue to face recurrent, perhaps
increasing, strains; but those who may hope to celebrate
its approaching demise, or decay into impotence, run the
risk of finding that they are a little previous.

6 · *Flashpoint in Katanga*

THE expansion of the Secretariat's executive role reached what seemed a flashpoint with the outbreak of the 'first battle of Katanga' on 13 September 1961.

Five days later, just across the border in Rhodesia, Dag Hammarskjöld was killed in a still unexplained air crash. The crisis that his death precipitated in New York, where a shocked Assembly met on 19 September, is already a matter of history. What concerns us here is one of its particular consequences.

Angry controversy already surrounded the action taken by the UN force in the Congo's Katanga province. The Rhodesian federal prime minister, Sir Roy Welensky, called it 'wanton and naked aggression against a simple people'. This charge was loudly echoed by many people, some simple and others less simple, in London, Paris, and Brussels – not all of them directly interested in the Katanga–Rhodesia mining complex. The anger throve on confusion and mis-information, partly the result of the deliberate fabrication of untruths, partly of innocent though sadly inaccurate reporting. (Reporting of the Katanga conflict was so bad as to disturb the International Press Institute. It also, apparently, seriously misled the British government, one of whose ministers, Lord Lansdowne, later conceded that 'many of the apparently more outrageous aspects of the United Nations' action as we had seen them in London were inaccurate or exaggerated'.)

Hammarskjöld's swift passage into silence left no single authoritative voice to speak for the UN as a whole against its accusers.

The accusations took, broadly, four forms. First, it was objected that the UN had no business to be getting into a fight at all.

Secondly, the UN was accused of intervening in a purely domestic political dispute.

Thirdly, the UN force was charged with committing atrocities.

Fourthly, the Secretariat was accused of being so anarchic that its representatives in the field could 'start a war' on their own initiative.

Significantly, when the second, and more violent, 'battle of Katanga' came in December 1961, the first three charges were levelled again, but little was heard of the fourth.

In the case of the September conflict, the fourth charge made it possible to denounce the UN action in spite of the awkward fact of the Secretary-General's massive reputation as both a dedicated and a diplomatic figure. The chief scapegoat chosen in Britain was Dr Conor Cruise O'Brien, the forty-four-year-old Irish diplomat, a veteran of half a dozen UN Assemblies, whom Hammarskjöld had recruited to the Secretariat in 1961 and sent to the Katanga as chief UN representative in June.

In a television interview after his resignation in December 1961, O'Brien said:

> The idea that I am personally responsible is one which was put out for political purposes, so as not to attack Mr Hammarskjöld directly.

His point had by then been reinforced by the outbreak, after his departure from the Katanga, of fighting on a larger scale than September's, in circumstances which gave the critics no chance to revive the charge of 'anarchy' in the Secretariat.

In September, however, the focusing of outraged feeling on O'Brien, whom the British Foreign Office had long regarded as a 'wild anti-colonial boy', and whom it had already been pressing Hammarskjöld to remove, confused the real issues nicely from the viewpoint of the UN's opponents. Fairly typical was Lord Colyton's* letter in *The Times* of 21 September, in which he flatly stated that the UN force

---

* Former Conservative M.P., as Henry Hopkinson; Minister of State, Colonial Affairs, 1952–5.

had 'engaged in a most reckless offensive operation without the knowledge of Mr Hammarskjöld, and apparently on the authority of a local civilian United Nations representative'. When challenged to substantiate this, Colyton backed down. But the legend of O'Brien's 'guilt' went on being assiduously fostered. The Foreign Office kept it up even after its own ministers' public statements had contradicted it (for instance, Lansdowne's statement on 18 October, quoted on page 140). In December the Foreign Office, while refusing to comment formally on O'Brien's resignation and his charges of British pressure, was still discreetly circulating the idea – to quote *The Times* of 4 December 1961 – that

Dr O'Brien naturally wished to show that the United Nations was getting on with the task of evacuating the mercenaries from Katanga. Just before Mr Hammarskjöld was due to visit the Congo, he decided to risk using United Nations forces in Elisabethville to round up the remaining mercenaries there.

As to the first of the four charges brought against the UN, the reader is referred to the discussion on page 18 of the unfounded notion that the organization should avoid violent conflict at all costs. What is relevant here is that the instinctive shock that many people felt at the sight of the 'peace force' in combat in September 1961 had a strong psychological effect. Specifically, it encouraged the tendency among people who knew little of the facts to assume that, if the UN had done anything so 'outrageous', the respected Secretary-General could not possibly have countenanced it. Such people were ready to accept the scapegoat that accusing fingers quickly indicated.

To deal with the other charges, it is necessary to go over the record of events, and to discuss some of the principal myths circulated about the UN action, and the origins of their circulation. The need to set out the elementary facts of an affair about which so much has been said and written may seem strange at first sight. But many of these facts have been smothered, both by deliberate misrepresentation and by the recoil from embarrassing truths that is often so instinctive as to be an unconscious act.

The reader's verdict must be his own. But he may fairly be asked to bear in mind just what it is that he is judging. Nobody – certainly not the UN's own servants, who have reason to know its limitations – is inviting him to find that the UN record in this case is flawlessly perfect. If the UN were really directed and manned by all-powerful archangels, the Katanga problem would presumably have been solved, in an ideal manner, as soon as it arose – without any argument. In the real world, the real questions are: What were the alternatives to UN action? If UN action was the best course, what might have been done to make it more effective? Why could these things not be done? And, above all, what lessons for the future of the UN are to be drawn from the Katanga experience?

The Katanga, richest of the Belgian Congo's six provinces, was about the size of France. The copper field along its southern fringe (the other half of the field lying in Rhodesia) provided a large share of the Congo revenues under Belgian rule. The Baluba, who occupy most of the north, are the biggest element in the total Katanga population of two million. In the south the Luanda are historically powerful, but the mining towns have drawn in a very mixed African work force, including many Baluba from Kasai province.

The highlands of southern Katanga, like Rhodesia's, are congenial to Europeans. Its mineral economy was developed and owned by an interlinked group of Brussels-based companies, chief among them the Union Minière du Haut-Katanga, in which the Belgian state and a British-Rhodesian company, confusingly named Tanganyika Concessions Ltd ('Tanks' for short), were two major stockholders. In 1961–2 three U.M.H.K. directors were British – Captain Charles Waterhouse, Lord Selborne, and Sir Ulick Alexander*. 'Tanks' owned all the debentures and ninety

* All three are Privy Councillors. Waterhouse, now chairman of 'Tanks', a Conservative M.P. from 1924 to 1945 and 1950–7, was a junior minister in 1928, 1931–6, and 1939–45, and successively Comptroller and Treasurer of H.M. Household in 1937–9.
Lord Selborne is Lord Salisbury's cousin and a Companion of

per cent of the equity of the Benguela Railway Company, whose line links the Katanga mining area with the port of Lobito in Portuguese Angola. U.M.H.K. reported net 1961 profits of 1,526,580,449 Belgian francs (about £10,900,000); 'Tanks' reported profits after taxation of £3,296,325; Benguela Railway's net 1961 operating receipts were £3,212,730.

Under Belgian rule Africans in the Katanga, as elsewhere in the Congo, had no chance of getting even a little political experience until the last months before independence came at the end of June 1960. In the first-ever elections, in May 1960, twenty-five seats out of sixty in the provincial assembly were won by the Conakat party, led by Moïse Tshombe, son-in-law of the Luanda paramount chief. The Balubakat party and its allies won twenty-two. Tshombe was accepted as provincial president, although the Balubakat boycott of the assembly had left it without a quorum.

Conakat's programme stressed a wide degree of provincial autonomy, but it had not openly advocated secession. In July 1960, however, as soon as the newly independent Congo's army mutinied and Belgium rushed troops back into the country, Tshombe declared Katanga an independent state.

Although not even Belgium ever recognized his 'state', he obtained massive Belgian support. U.M.H.K. paid over to his régime all the revenues – about £14,000,000 a year – that were legally due to the Congo government. With this wealth, Tshombe built up disproportionately large armed forces, as large as Nigeria's, and officered by regulars openly seconded from the Belgian army. (His backers also provided a munificent personal bank account in Switzerland, just in

Honour. A Conservative M.P. from 1920 to 1940, a junior minister in 1922–9, Minister of Economic Warfare 1942–5, he has been chairman of the National Provincial Bank and president of the Church Army.

Sir Ulick Alexander, G.C.B., G.C.V.O., C.M.G., O.B.E., became chairman of 'Tanks' in 1952 and a director of U.M.H.K. in 1954. Keeper of the Privy Purse, 1936–52, and later Extra Equerry to the Queen, he lived for some years in Salisbury, Rhodesia.

case.) These origins have to be borne in mind when one reads, for instance, the U.M.H.K. chairman's statement at the annual general meeting in May 1962, explaining why the company was still paying all revenues to Tshombe:

... this régime ... has shown on numerous occasions its capacity to impose its decisions. Union Minière cannot therefore do other than comply with the instructions of the Katangese authorities.

M. Gillet did not, understandably, recall that Tshombe's breakaway régime could never have acquired 'its capacity to impose its decisions' if the company had not filled its coffers at the start. In those early months, U.M.H.K. can hardly have felt itself helpless against Tshombe's might, for the effective military power in the Katanga was that of the Belgian army.

The return to the independent Congo of Belgian forces was, of course, the explicit reason for the appeal to the UN for military assistance made on 12 July 1960 by the Congo's president, Joseph Kasavubu, and prime minister, Patrice Lumumba. The withdrawal of these forces from the whole Congo – including by definition its Katanga province – was called for by the UN Security Council on 14 July, which also authorized Hammarskjöld to provide UN 'military assistance', and thus empowered him to create the UN force in the Congo. The Belgian foreign minister told the Council on 20 July that Belgian troops would withdraw as soon as enough UN troops to restore order arrived. But on 14 July Tshombe forbade the UN to send troops into 'his' province, and insisted that Belgian troops must stay there; and on 27 July the Belgian prime minister said the UN should 'not intervene in the Congo's internal affairs' in regard to the Katanga problem.

Backed by 1,700 Belgian soldiers, Tshombe announced on 3 August that UN troops 'will have to fight their way in'. Hammarskjöld sent Ralph Bunche to reason with him, in vain; Bunche reported back that he believed a UN entry would indeed mean a battle. Hammarskjöld called an emergency Council meeting and asked for a clarification of his mandate. Vasily Kuznetsov, the Soviet representative, tabled a resolution demanding that the UN force fight its way in, but withdrew it on finding no support. Belgium's delegate promised that its soldiers would not resist a UN entry. At the end of a twelve-hour session lasting until 4 a.m. on 9 August, the Council adopted a resolution presented by Mongi Slim of Tunisia and Sir Claude Corea of Ceylon.

This insisted on UN entry into, and the speedy removal of Belgian forces from, the Katanga. It also reaffirmed that the UN force would not intervene in any purely internal conflict. This was one of the ground rules for UN forces recommended by Hammarskjöld as far back as 1958, in a report on the experience of UNEF in the Suez–Sinai operations, and already twice tacitly approved by the Council in regard to the Congo, since he had stressed this rule in statements to it on 13 and 20 July, before it voted its first two empowering resolutions, and had not been challenged.

Tshombe then announced that he would admit the UN force, but only on conditions. Hammarskjöld told him there could be no conditions, only discussion of 'the modalities of deployment'.

On 12 August Hammarskjöld flew to Elisabethville with five planeloads of Swedish soldiers. While his white Convair circled the airfield, Tshombe, who had ringed the runway with machine-guns and armoured cars, was still trying to haggle by ground-to-air radio, demanding that the troop-carriers turn back. The Secretary-General landed in the ring of guns, resisted Tshombe's efforts to hustle him off in a waiting car, and watched his own men come in. The 220 Swedes at once took over control of the airport from the Belgian paratroopers, and next day over 1,000 more UN troops arrived in the province.

The UN was in. The Belgian troops duly left the Katanga during the following weeks.

Lumumba, however, encouraged by the Russians, bitterly reviled Hammarskjöld; refused to see him; accused him of failing to consult the Congo government before taking his action (in fact Hammarskjöld had consulted Antoine Gizenga, the vice-premier, and Justin Bomboko, the foreign minister, who were in New York, and who had approved his plans); claimed that the UN force should have been made to accept his orders to subdue Tshombe by force; and whipped up his followers to assault UN personnel in Leopoldville.

Hammarskjöld had neither a Council mandate, nor the consent of the states contributing to the UN force, for a fighting entry into the breakaway province. But it was easy for the Russians, who had by now decided to play their own game in the Congo, to exploit Lumumba's – and other people's – ignorance of the UN mechanism, and their frustration over the survival of Tshombe's régime. Hammarskjöld was personally billed as the accused in a smear campaign that eventually became one of the most venomous in history (greatly exceeding the one mounted against him by British 'Suez groupers' in 1956), and which took in a multitude of innocents, particularly after Lumumba's death at the hands of Tshombe's associates.

The tanglewood tale of the Congo's next twelve months cannot be told here even in outline. But it is relevant to recall Kasavubu's dismissal of Lumumba in September 1960 and subsequent acceptance of Colonel Mobutu's military take-over; Gizenga's proclamation in November, at Stanleyville, of a rival Congo 'government'; Hammarskjöld's tenacious insistence on a return to constitutional politics; his rejection of the claims made for the Kasavubu–Mobutu–Ileo régime by America and most of its allies, and of those made for Gizenga by Russia, Yugoslavia, Egypt, and other states; and his search, with the help of mainly Afro-Asian associates, for national reconciliation in the Congo, which was largely achieved in August 1961.

That year of veering confusion, during which each of the rival claimants for power in turn bit the UN's helping hand, helped Tshombe and his free-spending and influential propagandists to depict the Katanga as an 'oasis of peace' in a chaotic Congo.

The picture was false. True, U.M.H.K. carried on

happily and profitably, and European visitors to Elisabeth-ville were duly impressed by its outward calm. But even in 'E'ville' this 'peace' was achieved only by ruthless repres-sion, mainly executed by a Belgian-staffed political police under the authority of Godefroid Munongo, the 'minister of the interior'. Munongo, grandson of a Bayeke chief who had been a mighty man in the Katanga, quickly won a reputation as a far tougher man than his nominal leader, Tshombe, who more than once confessed that he could not control him.

In most of northern and central Katanga, Tshombe's writ did not even run, though his white-led troops campaigned there repeatedly, burning many villages and indulging in indiscriminate mass killing.

This continuing bloodshed in the Katanga was in marked contrast to the rest of the Congo, where, after the Kasai conflict in late August 1960 between Lumumba's troops and those of Albert Kalonji (another secessionist), the rival forces showed little more fighting zeal than Tweedledum and Tweedledee. As late as May 1961, on the other hand, the Tshombist troops' attempts to seize more territory in the north were, according to a report then issued by Hammarskjöld, creating a real danger of civil war, which was averted only by the UN urgently reinforcing its own strength in the area.

A Belgian colonel commanded these Tshombist troops, who were directed and stiffened by 350 other Belgian officers and N.C.O.s and at least a hundred newly recruited white mercenaries, largely French, Rhodesian, South African, and British.

Soldiers of fortune had little difficulty in entering the Katanga from Rhodesia (and re-entering, after the UN had deported them). Although Welensky repeatedly denied that his government was letting mercenaries cross into Katanga, he eventually conceded, in December 1961, that he could not stop illegal crossing; and his ministry of home affairs admitted even more revealingly, on 10 January 1962, just after it had allowed a fresh batch of mercenaries to go in to join Tshombe's forces, that the Rhodesian federal immigration laws 'do not concern themselves with what the traveller intends to do when he reaches his country of destination'.

Tshombe's continued dependence on foreign soldiers and political advisers was a direct defiance of the UN after 21 February 1961, when the Security Council demanded (France and Russia abstaining) the immediate withdrawal from the Congo of all foreign soldiers and political advisers not under UN control.

The 21 February resolution also urged the reconvening of the Congo parliament under UN protection. This was achieved in July, 200 out of 221 members attending (including anti-Tshombe members from the Katanga). On 2 August a coalition government led by Cyrille Adoula was approved by a virtually unanimous vote. Adoula's government was accepted by Kasavubu, by Mobutu, and by Gizenga, who on 7 August dissolved his own rival 'government', and agreed to serve as a deputy premier.

At last – thanks largely to the UN representatives' patient efforts for national reconciliation – the Congo had a legitimate, broadly based, and universally recognized government, and one that was prepared to cooperate with the UN.

The context of the problem of the Katanga mercenaries was thus transformed. Nobody was more keenly aware of this than Hammarskjöld, as is shown by Andrew Wilson's account, published in the *Observer* of 24 September 1961, of a talk with him in Leopoldville shortly before his fatal flight. Wilson reported Hammarskjöld's views thus:

He divided the whole Congo operation into two phases – the phase before the formation of a legally recognized government last August, and the phase that followed. During the first phase the UN was obliged to rely on negotiation and persuasion in its efforts to reunite the opposing factions.... With the formation of the Adoula government, the UN's duty to evict the Katanga mercenaries – a duty imposed by the Security Council resolution of last February and given a legal basis by the ordinance of Mr Adoula on 24 August – became 'inescapable'.

Immediately after 21 February, Hammarskjöld, working in almost daily consultation with the mainly Afro-Asian advisory committee on the Congo which he had set up in August 1960, had put what pressure he could on Tshombe and on the Belgian government to hasten the removal of the Katanga mercenaries and foreign advisers. But in May he had to report that the Belgian position 'still fell far short of what was required by the resolution'. As to Tshombe, he was still merrily recruiting; in April, UN troops intercepted and deported a party of no less than thirty newly enlisted mercenaries, mostly from Rhodesia and South Africa; others were caught during May.

There is no doubt that from February onward Hammarskjöld and his closest advisers were set on securing the removal of the mercenaries and political advisers at the earliest possible moment. They knew that the foreign soldiers and advisers were not merely sustaining Tshombe but effectively controlling him – and holding him back from coming to terms with the rest of the Congo, as he was at times personally inclined to do. They had a defence against the charge that the UN would be intervening in a purely domestic conflict; a defence against this charge had been laid down by Hammarskjöld on 12 August 1960, when he cited, for Lumumba's benefit, the Council's attitude in earlier cases involving both domestic and external elements, and reserved a UN right to intervene if an external element was used to influence the outcome of a domestic conflict. They saw no future for the Congo, for peace in Africa, or indeed for the sorely strained UN, if the Katanga deadlock was not broken.

Hammarskjöld secured the confidence of the new Kennedy administration in America. India, defying Khrushchev's public thunder, sent him 5,000 more troops. Nehru honourably maintained this crucial support even after Anglo–American hostility had forced the resignation of Rajeshwar Dayal,* the distinguished Indian diplomat who, as chief UN official in the Congo since mid September 1960,

* See note 1 on page 156.

had become the West's whipping-boy while Hammarskjöld became Russia's – although the two men had worked on exactly the same lines throughout.

Symbolically, as Dayal silently withdrew from UN service in May, O'Brien, Hammarskjöld's chosen emissary to a Katanga where the showdown was now imminent, joined the Secretariat. O'Brien was to meet much the same political fate as Dayal, but not to bear it with such diplomatic silence.*

Before taking up his duty in Elisabethville in mid June, O'Brien spent a fortnight in New York working with the Secretary-General's 'Congo Club' of official advisers, and was thus left in no doubt about Hammarskjöld's firm intention of ending the mercenary problem. Even after reaching the Katanga, however, he shared with most of his colleagues the hope that Tshombe and his backers, faced at last with a generally accepted national government and with a UN strengthened in both mandate and sinews, would prudently accept the February resolution.

Tshombe made gestures that kept such hopes alive a little longer. He let Conakat representatives attend the national parliament; he signed an agreement with Mobutu for military 'integration'. But the representatives were recalled and the agreement was stillborn. Tshombe rejected UN offers of safe conduct if he would go to see Adoula. In August Munongo and the European directors of Tshombe's 'ministry of information' started to build up yet another 'hate' campaign against the UN.

On 24 August the new Congo government issued an *ordonnance* providing for the expulsion of Tshombe's mercenaries, and Adoula formally requested UN aid in ensuring its execution. This decree, as Hammarskjöld told Wilson in the interview already quoted (and as Dr Sture Linner, the

---

* O'Brien's statements after he resigned in December 1961, and his book, *To Katanga and Back*, published late in 1962, were so outspoken that, although he vigorously exposed the false claims of Tshombe's backers, they in turn hailed some of his revelations as confirming their charges against the UN.

chief UN official in the Congo since Dayal's departure, noted in his report of 14 September) provided a clear legal basis, in terms of the Congo constitution, for UN action to evict the mercenaries.

The citing of the ordinance by the UN, and other instances of the government and the UN cooperating in regard to the Katanga, have been triumphantly 'exposed' by some critics as evidence of 'furtive collusion' between them – sometimes as evidence of collusion between Adoula and local UN officials behind Hammarskjöld's back. Both versions are false. There was nothing wrong about the UN thus co-operating with (though not taking orders from) the univers-ally recognized government of the territory on which it was acting – and the UN was now blessed with a cooperative Congo government.

'Collusion' was to be particularly 'detected' in the arrival at Elisabethville, late on 13 September, of Egyde Bocheley-Davidson, the government's appointed representa-tive in the province. (The constitution provides for such a representative in each province, but the Katanga post had, understandably, not been filled.) That morning, as later pages will show, Tshombe had at first reacted to the UN's move by agreeing to cooperate; having then failed to restrain the fighting zeal of his white warriors and effective masters, he had fled, or been taken, to the Rhodesian border; and the driving wheels of his régime, the foreign-run political police and propaganda apparatuses, had been stopped by spokes inserted by the UN. At the time, it seemed that the secessionist régime had come to an end.

As has been noted already, the UN Secretariat had long ago perceived that the removal of the foreign elements – military and political – that sustained the secessionist régime and controlled its essentials meant that the régime would cease to exist. Whether, in such a situation, Tshombe chose to cooperate (as the UN hoped) or to vanish, the effect of removing the 'external element' would be to bring his realm 'within the framework of the Congo'. It was the government's right and duty to establish its proper constitutional representation in the province in these circumstances.

Another allegation* is that Hammarskjöld was 'betrayed' by his subordinates in this matter. In fact, he knew of Bocheley-Davidson's appointment in advance. He and they had vainly urged the Congo government to choose a representative better suited for a post which, as they saw it, would involve cooperation with Tshombe, if he broke free from the 'wild men'.

To return to 24 August: with the *ordonnance* behind it, the UN lost no more time. There was none to be lost. The Elisabethville radio was busily whipping up hate and fear. Munongo was uttering violent menaces and inflammatory falsehoods, such as his 'announcement', on 26 August, that the UN was already flying 1,500 Congo government troops to Elisabethville. His political police and Bayeke gangs were threatening, arresting, and beating up the 'disloyal' (that is, anti-secessionist) Africans of Elisabethville, who began to flock to the UN force's camps, begging for protection.

Early on 28 August, the UN troops in Elisabethville took over the radio station, the telegraph office, and other key points, surrounded Munongo's residence, and, having thus reduced the risk of a violent reaction being organized, began to round up the mercenaries and the overt and covert foreign advisers on their 'wanted' list. (Many of the civilian names on the list had been agreed with Tshombe, and with the Belgian government. It did not include technicians who had refrained from playing a political role in support of secession.)

There was no resistance from Tshombe's forces. Many of the 500 wanted men were quickly rounded up, and their evacuation was put in hand.

One must consider here: what if there had been resistance that day? If fighting had broken out on 28 August, it would

* Made, for example, in a 'report' published in 1962, from 79 Madison Avenue, by the 'American Committee for Aid to Katanga Freedom Fighters'. The ignorance of the author (a professor) on this point indicates the general quality of a report which sympathizers hailed as 'a gruesome catalogue of crimes committed by UN troops'.

have been difficult for the UN's antagonists even to launch, let alone sustain, the idea that Hammarskjöld could never have countenanced the use of force. There is no doubt that he consciously faced the possibility of fighting when he approved the 28 August action – though he, and O'Brien and other UN officials, sincerely hoped to evict the mercenaries by a swift and bloodless operation.

That operation – code-named 'Rumpunch' – had been begun and proved bloodless. But 'Rumpunch' was halted almost at once, by pressure upon the UN by the representatives of a group of European governments, including Britain.

Tshombe, for his part, accepted the seemingly inevitable. O'Brien reassured him early on 28 August about the UN's intentions. Tshombe broadcast, at midday, an announcement that

the United Nations is at present engaged in withdrawing military personnel of foreign nationality serving in the Katanga forces. The government bows to the decisions of the United Nations. ... I ask you all to go on working and keep calm. ...

The Africans of Katanga kept quite calm; and Tshombe's African soldiers cheerfully accepted the dismissal of all their foreign officers.

Calm, however, was not universal. The Belgian, British, and French consuls in Elisabethville urgently called upon the UN to stop the round-up. Similar pressure was brought to bear on the UN at higher levels by their governments.*

The Belgian consul, backed by his British and French colleagues, undertook, if the round-up was halted, to ensure that all the wanted men duly surrendered and were evacuated. The consuls also demanded that the UN detach troops to protect Europeans who, they claimed, now felt themselves in dire peril in other mining towns, particularly Jadotville.†

* See notes 2, 3, and 4 on pages 157–8.

† The Europeans of 'Tshombe's' Katanga were often oddly quick to switch abruptly from reviling the UN for meddling in their 'oasis of multiracial harmony', to begging it to save them from the Africans.

The undertaking to ensure the surrender of all the wanted men was not honoured. The demand for the garrisoning of Jadotville turned out to lead to a well-planned trap.

With misgivings, the UN yielded to these pressing representations. It halted the search for the white men on its black list. It sent an Irish company to Jadotville.

Elisabethville was very quiet on 29 August. The hate campaign had been shut off like a tap. The consular staffs were apparently working hard on repatriation arrangements. Tshombe was supposed to be appealing to the mercenaries for calm and cooperation.

On 30 August Welensky violently denounced the UN action and publicly assured Tshombe of the Rhodesian federal government's support in resisting it. (Britain, it may be recalled, was constitutionally responsible for federated Rhodesia's external relations.)

Next day the British consul in Elisabethville, Denzil Dunnett,* and his vice-consul, David Smith, an official of the Rhodesian federal service, went to see Tshombe, whose newspapers promptly 'splashed' the story that these officials had personally conveyed Sir Roy Welensky's pledges of support to him. They had.†

Newly emboldened, the hate propagandists swung quickly back into action with a still more violent wave of incitement against 'disloyal' Africans as well as against the UN staff. Terrorized Baluba, Chokwe, and other Elisabethville Africans flooded to the UN camps. By 5 September the UN had 25,000 of them on its hands; by 9 September,

* There should be no supposition that Dunnett at any time acted in any way contrary to his instructions. In June 1962 he was given an O.B.E.

† Sir Roy, who officially deplored the Katanga secession, once also said: 'This country of mine can play little or no part in deciding the outcome of events in Katanga.' Such modest discretion, however, did not always mark his words, or those of his officials. His High Commissioner in London, Albert Robinson (since knighted), in a letter to *The Economist* published on 20 January 1962, described 'the survival of a stable pro-Western government in Elisabethville' as 'vital to the [Rhodesian] Federation'.

35,000. Huddled together in destitution, they preferred even this to facing Munongo's thuggery.

O'Brien later commented that

it is one of the most remarkable achievements of the Katangese propaganda machine that it has been able to use the existence of the refugees to discredit not the people from whom they fled, but the people who gave them protection.

One may note here Sir William Teeling's reference in the House of Commons in March 1962 to '30,000 Baluba tribesmen whom the UN have pushed into the equivalent of a concentration camp'. Apart from the fact that the appalled UN neither pushed nor pulled them, some 16,000 of the camp refugees were not Baluba, though it suited the propagandists to pretend they all were.*

O'Brien pressed Tshombe – in vain – to call off the terrorism and to suspend Munongo, who, with the white 'ultras', was responsible for it. When Tshombe revealed that he could not control them, O'Brien gave him written warning that the UN might have to act under the February resolution's provision for the use of force.

The ninth of September was the deadline by which the consuls were required to ensure the surrender of all the wanted men. But, when it came, many of the most dangerous were still at large, and actively fomenting trouble. They had resumed effective command of Tshombe's African troops, in spite of his nominally final dismissal of all foreign officers on 28 August. They were arming European civilian sympathizers and organizing them for combat.

On 8 September the Irish company that had been sent to Jadotville, at the insistence of the European consuls and their governments, to protect supposedly imperilled Europeans, found itself surrounded by greatly superior forces – led by Europeans.

* Lord Russell of Liverpool, in a pamphlet issued in April 1962, called the refugee camp 'a white elephant for which the UN has only itself to blame'. Oddly, on another page he wrote of 'a reign of terror against the Baluba living in the *communes* of Elisabethville' – without, apparently, seeing any conflict between the two statements.

On the same day UN representatives in Brussels urgently asked the Belgian government to order its Elisabethville consular staff to honour their undertaking. Whatever orders Brussels sent, the consulate's response was to act even more openly as a centre for the organizing of the anti-UN campaign.

In Elisabethville, O'Brien formally reminded the consuls of the deadline, and warned them that if the mercenaries were not evacuated immediately the UN would be compelled – in the words of Linner's subsequent report – 'to resume action for implementing the 21 February resolution by all means at its disposal'.

He was by now recommending to his own superiors that, in this quickly worsening situation, the action broken off on 28 August on assurances that had proved worthless should be resumed without more delay and with decisive firmness. On 11 September Linner sent to Elisabethville two of his senior colleagues in Leopoldville, Khiary and Fabry. Mahmoud Khiary, an impressively large and agile-minded Tunisian, was Linner's principal political affairs official, and often served as his deputy. He had played a valuable part, together with Robert Gardiner of Ghana and other UN men, in securing the national reconciliation that had brought parliament back to life in July and created the Adoula coalition government. Vladimir Fabry, an American whose dry lawyer's mind was something of a foil for Khiary's, was chief UN legal counsel in the Congo. A week later he was to die with Hammarskjöld.

After consultations, O'Brien and Brigadier K. A. S. Raja, the Indian commander of UN troops in the Katanga, and their staffs were given instructions for operation 'Morthor', which was to be carried out on 13 September if Tshombe spurned a last appeal. This time there could not be as successful a surprise action as on 28 August; and, when asked about the likelihood of violent resistance, the opinion they gave was that a certain amount might be unavoidable, but that it ought not to last long. This view was to prove over-confident; but less wildly so than was commonly said at the time. Even though Tshombe, hustled off by his 'advisers', was not to fulfil the UN's expectation that he would once again, as on 28 August, broadcast an appeal for cooperation, few of his African soldiers showed much enthusiasm for fighting in his name – although they had the advantage of the UN force in both numbers and equipment.

What the UN executive did not foresee was how skilfully an international propagandist machine could build up a picture of it attempting a 'punitive war' (Lord Lansdowne's phrase) and being 'defeated' by 'Africans'. The reality, throughout the week of intermittent conflict that followed the UN force's move on 13 September, was that it was firing only when attacked, and often not responding even then (being anxious, in particular, not to imperil civilian life) to harassing fire that came mainly from European properties, in Elisabethville's European quarters, much of it coming visibly from civilian-dressed Europeans. Nor did the UN, in spite of its forebodings, fully foresee its adversaries' skilful exploitation of the Jadotville trap – where, again, the African Tshombist troops showed no wish to fight, and it was only the 'imperilled' Europeans who bombarded the Irish company, and eventually reduced it by cutting off its water.

All levels in the UN executive hoped for another bloodless operation, as on 28 August. The orders were to reassure the African Tshombist troops that the UN had no intention of disarming them, and to do everything possible to avoid a clash with them.

At the same time, the second UN action again implied a conscious decision to face the possibility of fighting, as on 28 August. As to the sponsors of the idea of 'a reckless offensive operation without the knowledge of Mr Hammarskjöld', some of them may have been partially enlightened – a month later – by none other than the British Foreign Under-Secretary, Lord Lansdowne, who was sped to the

Congo on 15 September to impress Hammarskjöld with his government's indignation, and with the implicit consequences if the UN did not at once back down.*

Lansdowne thus described† his talk with Hammarskjöld in Leopoldville on 16 September:

Mr Hammarskjöld then explained to me the origins of the UN actions on 13 September. He said that in the opinion of his officers on the spot it was necessary to act urgently against the remaining foreign mercenaries in Katanga. The operation of 28 August, which had been endorsed by Mr Tshombe, had been only partially successful. Intimidation against the UN had been increasing.... There was a danger that with the assistance of these foreigners an organized underground movement might be built up.

Mr Hammarskjöld made it clear to me that the object of the action of 13 September was to complete the work of 28 August. ... He fully accepted responsibility for the action that they [his officers] had taken.... It is my conviction that he spoke with absolute frankness. ...

When the morning of 13 September came, Hammarskjöld himself was on his way to the Congo. Some days earlier he had suggested to Adoula that he should be invited to Leopoldville, and on 10 September he had formally accepted Adoula's invitation. He left New York on 12 September in the hope that Tshombe might respond to a last approach that would make it unnecessary to resort to military methods again. For, on that day, Khiary and O'Brien once more – in vain – asked Tshombe to stop the hate propaganda and terrorism and to give an assurance that the foreign advisers and soldiers would be promptly evacuated. They once more – in vain – offered him safe conduct if he would go to Leopoldville; this time, the invitation was to go there to meet Hammarskjöld.

As this final bid yielded nothing, the UN forces moved again, at 4 a.m. on 13 September, to take over the Elisabethville radio station and telegraph office, and, this time, the

---

* See note 5 on page 158.
† In the House of Lords on 18 October.

Belgian-run political police HQ and the residences of other 'ministers' as well as Munongo's – although the UN rightly doubted that Munongo would be caught a second time.

But the period of grace extended by the UN under diplomatic pressure had been long enough for the hard-core mercenaries, chief among them a French ex-officer from Algeria, Réné Faulques, to prepare a thorough military plan.

Picked companies of 'paracommandos' trained and indoctrinated by Faulques at Shinkolobwe camp had been placed at several of the points the UN force had orders to take over. They fought it out – although there is evidence (hotly denied in Brussels) that even this amount of conflict with African troops might have been avoided, if sniping from the Belgian consulate building had not shattered what was, till then, a peaceful parley with the garrison of the telegraph office, whom the UN troops were reassuring that they were not going to be disarmed.

Once firing had thus begun, snipers opened up from private houses and other positions in the European quarters. The UN troops, having secured their key-point objectives in the first three hours of action, thereafter confined themselves to defence. Repeated assaults on their positions were led by mercenary officers. Europeans directed mortar and machine-gun fire against the densely packed African refugee camp, and against the radio station when it broadcast appeals for calm, as well as against UN positions and offices. The mercenaries and local European civilians – including doctors – used vehicles marked with the Red Cross to transport arms and ammunition; in some cases bazooka shells were fired from these 'ambulances'. (All these methods were again used in the December fighting.)

The African quarters of Elisabethville remained calm and quiet. Nor did the UN encounter African hostility anywhere else in the Katanga, except where there were foreigners to lead attacks on it. White-led troops assailed UN positions at Albertville and Kamina, and the trapped Irish company at Jadotville was shelled and underwent repeated attacks; it captured two Belgians who led the assault on 14 September.

On that day a jet aircraft flown from Kolwezi by a Belgian living in South Africa named Joseph Delin began to strafe and bomb UN positions from Elisabethville to Kamina. Delin attacked a UN hospital plane evacuating wounded, and destroyed aircraft on the ground. The UN, having no fighters of its own, had to limit transport flights to hours of darkness. (This was why Hammarskjöld's fatal flight was made at night, by a long circuitous route, and with some attempt, not wholly effective, to preserve secrecy.)

The week-long fighting was a one-sided affair, for the UN, as Hammarskjöld pointed out in his message to Tshombe on 17 September, was firing only when attacked. Nor, it seems, was Tshombe personally at all eager for a fight. He was simply overruled by his 'advisers' – although he afterwards took all the credit he could for 'Katanga's victory over the UN'.

Only a few minutes after the first shots, Tshombe, speaking with O'Brien by telephone, agreed that the UN should be allowed to complete its task without further resistance. He agreed to broadcast another appeal for cooperation with the UN. Apparently he did at first try to order an immediate cease-fire, but the mercenaries took no notice. A UN official who, at Tshombe's request, drove to his presidential palace to pick him up was fired on at the gates and had to retire quickly. At about 6 a.m. Tshombe vanished. It was learnt afterwards that at about that time he spent an hour at Dunnett's house, but neither he nor the consul got in touch with the UN. Later he was reported near the Rhodesian border, where Munongo too had retreated.

O'Brien went on trying to contact him and arrange a cease-fire, with some help from Tshombe's adjutant and his 'vice-president', Kibwe. On 15 September Tshombe and Kibwe agreed to meet O'Brien at the British consulate, but failed to appear. Kibwe subsequently told Dunnett that Tshombe had been on the point of going to this meeting when he was stopped by his 'advisers'.

Meanwhile Hammarskjöld, in Leopoldville, had gone over the records of the decisions taken by his officials before his arrival, and of the information on which those decisions had been based, and had reviewed the situation with them at length. His eventual comment was that he would have taken the same decisions if he had been in Leopoldville himself.

Before 13 September was over, however, Hammarskjöld was made only too vividly aware that the new UN action had aroused reactions even more angry than those that the move on 28 August had evoked – British reactions being much the most significant. Welensky had ordered Rhodesian troops and bombers to the border, and his loud denunciations of the new UN action had been echoed by many voices in London, where the government announced that day that it was sending Lansdowne to the Congo.

Within a few hours of Hammarskjöld's arrival there, he came under urgent pressure from the British ambassador, Derek Riches. According to one detailed account, Riches, acting on direct instructions from Lord Home, warned the Secretary-General that if he could not promise that the fighting would be swiftly ended, or explain the Katanga events to the satisfaction of the British government, all British support for the UN Congo operation might be withdrawn.*

Hammarskjöld needed no urging to seek a cease-fire; the UN had sought one from the start. But he was not prepared to back down unconditionally.

Lansdowne has disclosed that, when he went to Hammarskjöld on 16 September and delivered a lengthy onslaught on the UN action – based, by his own account, on inaccurate information which the Secretary-General patiently corrected for him – he found Hammarskjöld already planning to invite Tshombe to meet him. Around midnight that night, the elusive Tshombe sent to O'Brien, through Dunnett, a

* Arthur Gavshon, *The Last Days of Dag Hammarskjöld*. Gavshon is a diplomatic correspondent for the Associated Press. (See also note 5 on page 158).

proposal that they should meet in Rhodesia. O'Brien at once informed Hammarskjöld, who promptly passed back, along the same channel, his own offer to meet Tshombe.

His long message emphasized that he was not offering to meet to discuss a cease-fire: he stipulated a cease-fire before the meeting. The meeting would be to discuss 'a solution of the present conflict within the framework established by the Security Council and already accepted by you ... thus opening the way to a solution of the Katanga problem within the framework of the Congo'. Tshombe was reminded that he had already accepted the UN objectives: the removal of mercenaries and political advisers, and a political solution 'within the framework of the Constitution of the Congo Republic'.

At 10 a.m. on 17 September Dunnett gave O'Brien Tshombe's reply, which demanded, as conditions for a cease-fire, that the UN confine all its troops to their camps and stop all movement of reinforcements. This would mean their giving up the points they had occupied on 13 September, and their isolation in separate units which could be easily cut off not only from each other but also from their supply lines.

Hammarskjöld's response was to cable O'Brien:

Kindly inform Tshombe that the Secretary-General finds it impossible to accept the conditions for a cease-fire and a meeting. ... There can be no question of anything but an unconditional cease-fire. ...

When O'Brien asked Dunnett to pass this on, the consul told him that Tshombe was already about to leave for Ndola, just across the border in Rhodesia. On learning of this, Hammarskjöld decided to fly to Ndola himself despite the absence of any cease-fire agreement.

He did not see this as a humiliating 'journey to Canossa'. He had not felt he was compromising the UN by going to Peking in 1955, or by visiting Verwoerd in 1960 – though both these journeys had evoked doubt and criticism; in 1956–7 he had kept in touch with both Nasser and Ben

Gurion; he had tried to get to Budapest to see Kadar in December 1956. Nor was he travelling on his knees. His two messages to Tshombe do not suggest that he meant to disavow the UN's aims or actions, or to sue for peace.

Six hours' flight brought his aircraft over Ndola airport just after midnight, 17–18 September. A few minutes later and nine miles west of the airport, the four-engined DC6B, its landing wheels already lowered, and apparently completing its turn on to the normal line of approach for landing, hit the tops of trees in a thickly wooded area, ploughed forward for over 200 yards, broke up, and was engulfed in blazing fuel. The only one of the sixteen persons on board found alive never regained full consciousness and died three days later.

The crash, although exhaustively investigated by the Rhodesian authorities and by a UN commission, remains unexplained. The night was clear and calm, the three Swedish pilots experienced and fit, the aircraft had just undergone thorough inspection. It was in radio-telephone contact with Ndola airport for forty-five minutes as it approached, giving and obtaining routine landing data, and was seen in normal flight by many people just before it crashed. No evidence was found to sustain any of the theories advanced about sabotage, attack from either the air or the ground, or pilot error. The UN commission, reporting in April 1962, in effect returned an open verdict, while remarking critically on the Rhodesian authorities' delay in organizing a search (the wreck was not located until fifteen hours after the crash).

Early on 19 September Linner sent Khiary to Ndola, where he arranged with Tshombe for a cease-fire. From the beginning, the Tshombe forces violated the terms in almost every way possible. Their intransigence had been strengthened by their new confidence that they had powerful friends who would restrain UN action to carry out the February resolution; by the uncertainty that the fighting, the outcry in Britain and elsewhere, and Hammarskjöld's death had produced in the UN executive; and by their ability to use the Irish soldiers trapped at Jadotville as pawns. (They were eventually exchanged on 25 October.)

Tshombe met fresh UN demands for removal of foreign mercenaries with bland statements that they had all been dismissed; but several hundred remained, actively organizing his forces. In October British, Belgian, and French pilots flew a number of Dorniers from Germany to airfields controlled by the mercenaries, who then used them to bomb Kasai until the UN warned them off.

Ethiopia, Nigeria, and Sudan asked for a Security Council meeting on the Katanga situation. The Council met on 13 November. By then violent incitement against the UN was again mounting in Elisabethville.

The resolution adopted on 24 November (by nine to nil; Britain and France abstained) insisted on an immediate end to 'the secessionist activities illegally carried out by the provincial administration of Katanga, with the aid of external resources and manned by foreign mercenaries'. And it authorized the Secretary-General

to take vigorous action, including the use of requisite measure of force, if necessary, for the immediate apprehension, detention pending legal action and/or deportation of all foreign military and paramilitary personnel and political advisers not under the UN Command, and mercenaries as laid down in paragraph A-2 of the resolution of February 21.

For Britain, Sir Patrick Dean told the Council that this went 'dangerously far in encouraging the local command to use an added measure of force'. He served warning that continued British support of the Congo operation 'must depend upon the skill and wisdom and the conciliatory manner with which the UN carries out its mandate'.

U Thant, Acting Secretary-General since 3 November, making his first-ever statement to the Council, said he would carry out 'with determination and vigour' the task entrusted to him in the resolution, while also promising that the UN would 'redouble its attempts to achieve reconciliation, by peaceful means'.

Union Minière stock fell sharply.

Tshombe and his associates at once launched a campaign of even more inflammatory incitement to violent attacks on UN personnel. On 28 November George Ivan Smith, who had temporarily succeeded O'Brien as chief UN official in the Katanga, and Brian Urquhart, his deputy, were brutally beaten up with rifle butts by a gang of Faulques's 'para-commandos' after being dragged out of a private house where they had been invited to meet the American Senator Thomas Dodd, whom Tshombe later called 'one of our fervent champions'. In the next few days many UN personnel were assaulted, wounded or killed by shots, or abducted. It later became clear that a dozen had been deliberately seized to be exploited as hostages.

From 2 December white-led Tshombist troops began to put road blocks in a pattern that cut the UN units off from each other and from the airport. Two of the UN's battalions were being relieved that week, so that it was at a military disadvantage. Ivan Smith and Urquhart obtained promises that the blocks would be removed; instead, they were strengthened, and other visible preparations were made for the all-out attack on the UN for which Tshombe's associates had now publicly called.

On 5 December the UN force cleared the block on the airport road, with explicit authority from Thant to take all action necessary to restore its freedom of movement. Mortar and machine-gun fire from European houses was then directed upon UN positions, mercenary-piloted aircraft dropped bombs, and, as in September, the crowded refugee camp was heavily fired upon. The refugees suffered 170 casualties, and the UN had to allot much of its strength both to protecting them and to preventing them from avenging these cold-blooded killings.

The two weeks' fighting in December was fiercer and wider than September's. Although the UN troops once again fought under severe restraint, Faulques's strategy was clearly to make the city of Elisabethville itself the main battleground, and it was thus impossible to avoid all risk to civilian lives and property. The UN – contrary to many

Press reports – dropped no bombs; but UN aircraft used cannon and rocket fire against military targets, including, at the end, the Union Minière installations in Elisabethville, from which heavy mortar fire was still being poured on UN units even after an apparently chastened Tshombe had left for talks with Adoula at Kitona.

As in September, there were again loud denunciations of the UN in Britain when fighting began. The government, however, was noticeably slower to move for a cease-fire. Adlai Stevenson had promptly announced full American support for the UN action. Ivan Smith, an Australian widely known in London, and Urquhart, a British ex-officer with a fine war record, were awkward targets for a smear campaign such as had been directed against O'Brien. Thant who backed them to the hilt from the start, had been elected to office barely a month before, with British support. O'Brien, who had resigned from UN service – under pressure – and from the Irish diplomatic service 'in order to recover my freedom of speech and action', had published on 3 December a charge that Britain and France had been pressing for his removal since August (which was true); and that one of their aims had been

to bring home to all servants of the Organization that, whatever resolutions of the Security Council may say, it is unwise to apply them if these Powers do not wish them to be applied. ... If my resignation and consequent publicity make it even a little harder for these members of the Council to obstruct the implementation of the Council's new resolution also, and thereby to wreck the UN action in the Congo, then my resignation will have been worthwhile.

Between the right-wing and Rhodesian fury at the UN action, and the forces at home and abroad that supported it, the British government was caught in a cross-fire. On 7 December it agreed to supply bombs for UN use against hostile airfields: on 11 December it said it would not release them until UN policy was clarified. (As UN policy had just been clarified by Thant, the government had to make dubious use of garbled Press reports to sustain this position.)

On 13 December Britain at last called for a cease-fire. Thant replied that a cease-fire, before the UN's security and freedom of movement had been restored, 'would be a serious setback'. But the cease-fire call served to close the Conservative ranks for the 14 December Commons debate on a motion of confidence. In this debate the Leader of the Opposition, Hugh Gaitskell, dealt succinctly with the 'atrocity' charges that were once more being brought against the UN:

> Hon. Members opposite ... swallow any old atrocity story they get hold of. Do they realize that every single one of these stories has been denied? Where do they get these stories from? ... We all know perfectly well that a stream of lies and propaganda has been poured out by public relations experts employed for this purpose.

His challenge received no response.

The Katanga fighting in 1961, as we have seen (pages 10–11), gave rise to the wildest charges against the UN yet made in Britain. It was said to have 'tasted blood' and to be getting involved in 'a war of conquest'. The falsity of such charges was amply shown in the months that followed December's 'second battle of Katanga'. Although the UN force had visibly and decisively won the battle that had been thrust upon it, this military success was not simply followed through with military action. Instead, the UN patiently pursued the more frustrating aim of effecting the agreed objective of Congolese reunion without any more bloodshed.

Tshombe was given not just one last chance, but a whole series of chances, to come to terms with the Congo government. But the twelve months after December 1961 only revealed at wearisome length that his promises were as hollow as before, and his backers still uncompromisingly bent on keeping the Katanga mineral wealth in their hands. On 21 December at Kitona, after talks with Adoula, Tshombe had ostensibly accepted an agreement on re-union. Six months later, after he had twice spent a month haggling in Leopoldville (confidently accepting assurances of safe conduct from the same UN that he still periodically accused of hatching fiendish conspiracies against him), he was still stalling so hard that virtually nothing had been done to carry out the Kitona agreement.

At the same time, his international backers were, if anything, exerting themselves harder than ever in the propaganda field in the first half of 1962. The Union Minière was still financing his régime. Some hard-core mercenaries (including Faulques) had left the Katanga, but others had come in from Rhodesia in 1962, some of them without bothering much about secrecy. (In January, Thant's proposal to Britain that UN observers should watch the Rhodesian border-crossing points was rejected: by Welensky.)

In late June 1962 Tshombe broke off his talks with Adoula in a way that made it clear that he had no intention of coming to terms. In July Thant was moved to comment that Tshombe 'seemed to be playing for time' and showing 'obvious bad faith'. He formally appealed to all UN member governments to do what they could for a peaceful settlement, adding that if persuasion failed he had in mind a resort to economic pressure on the Tshombe régime.

Thant visited several European capitals in July, and talked with, among others, Macmillan about the Congo. In August he visited Russia – which, as before, was simultaneously demanding that the UN force should simply launch an all-out attack on the Tshombist troops, and refusing to contribute a single copeck to the UN operation for which it had voted. (The Russians invited him to record a broadcast for Moscow radio, and then, without notifying him, censored it. They cut out, in particular, his polite but pointed remark: 'I beg to be excused for saying that the Russian people do not fully understand the true character of the Congo problem'.) When the Assembly met in September, *Pravda* threateningly revived Khrushchev's 'troika' plan for abolishing Thant's office and fettering the Secretariat (page 39). Thant remained calm; and Russia, again finding no backers for its plan, eventually had to go along with the mass of Assembly members in voting on 30 November to give Thant a definitive term as Secretary-General running to November 1966.

Clearly, however, nothing that would help break the Congo deadlock could be expected from the Security Council. In fact the Council, so often wrongly supposed to be the UN's 'executive' organ, did not even meet once to discuss the Congo during 1962. Thant had to get along on the basis of the authority given in its resolution of November 1961; to have asked for its approval of any really specific and practical plan of action might have evoked Soviet, British, and French vetoes. The Secretary-General was forced to go ahead on his own. In August he put forward a detailed programme for Congolese national reconciliation, which became known as 'the U Thant plan'.

As might have been expected, Tshombe professed to accept the plan, and the machinery of mixed commissions to discuss implementation was again started up. But by November Gardiner, then head of the UN Congo operation, was compelled to report formally that Tshombe had once more blocked all actual progress, even in regard to the ousting of mercenaries. Thant gave further warning that the only non-violent way of effecting the UN's aims was by putting economic pressure on Tshombe and his backers; at the same time, foreseeing that their reaction might be to resort to violence, he asked member states to help bring the UN force up to full strength. Responses to his appeal came from countries ranging from Norway, Sweden, and Italy to Indonesia and the Philippines. (When Italy promised aircraft, Munongo's strong-arm men kidnapped the Italian consul in Elisabethville and shanghaied him into a complaisant Rhodesia.)

Tshombe continued to ignore, or answer with bland evasions, Gardiner's repeated appeals, warnings, and reminders. The Congo government asked all countries that were buying minerals from the Katanga to boycott it until Tshombe came to terms, and Thant publicly supported this request. He also asked Britain, France, Portugal, and South Africa in particular, as the states most directly assisting the

Tshombe régime, to help induce it to share the mineral revenues with the Congo government. The United States, after a few weeks of rather confused search for a compromise formula acceptable to Britain, declared its 'full support for the U Thant plan' and, jointly with Belgium, proclaimed that 'severe economic measures' would be necessary if Tshombe did not give way at once. On 30 November 1962 the Foreign Office got as far as stating that, if UN sanctions were applied, Britain 'would not seek to prevent their application'.

The Union Minière dropped various hints that it was at last going to start paying up some of the taxes it owed to the Congo government, and that it was sending representatives to Leopoldville to discuss this. Somehow they never turned up there. Tshombe and his friends dropped something louder than hints to the effect that they would blow up everything of value in the Katanga if the UN tried to push them at all hard. Even in Belgium these threats tended to blur the image of Tshombe as the only trustworthy protector of the Katanga investments. Paul-Henri Spaak, the Belgian foreign minister, described him as 'a mere rebel'. (Home, on the other hand, showed no diminution of deference toward him, and Welensky went on confabulating with him.) America agreed to carry out airlift operations in support of the UN, and, on 18 December, to help fill some important gaps in the equipment of its Congo force.

The UN approach was, quite visibly, to build up a show of strength that should convince the saner elements in the Tshombe régime that it would be useless to start another battle. What the Secretariat sought was not a showdown – in the sense of violent conflict – but a 'show-up', a bloodless confrontation (such as O'Brien had achieved, with Hammarskjöld's blessing, on 28 August 1961) that would finally make the Tshombists see the necessity of cooperating with the UN. But the saner elements, if any, were not in control in Elisabethville, where, instead of concessions, what developed was yet another series of unprovoked attacks on and abductions of UN soldiers and civilians, and another hate-propaganda campaign, accompanied by the destroying of bridges and building of new road blocks to entrap the UN forces.

On Christmas Eve, the Tshombist troops opened fire for no known reason, and kept it up for five hours despite UN efforts to get it stopped. A UN helicopter was shot down and its unarmed crew savagely beaten; one died. On Christmas Day there was further unprovoked firing. Still the UN troops refrained from firing a shot. The firing was mainly concentrated on the UN's Ethiopian units, presumably because those who directed it, perhaps influenced by their own propaganda tales about the Ethiopians being alarmingly ill-disciplined, hoped to provoke them into counter-action which could then be exploited as evidence that the UN was the 'aggressor'. They failed; the Ethiopians, with exemplary discipline, held their fire even after suffering casualties.

On the night of 27 December the one-sided firing and mortar shelling of UN positions became more widespread, and inflicted a growing number of casualties. All UN units continued to hold their fire. Tshombe at last, after being invited to tour the area to see with his own eyes that it was only his troops who were shooting, admitted that this was so, in the presence of the American and British consuls. Several times during hours of vain negotiation that dragged on through the next day he promised to stop the firing; but in the end he refused to sign a cease-fire order. The UN's representative and force commander told him that they must now act; their men, under continuous fire, were already having to withdraw from some exposed positions.

Then, after four days of complete restraint, the UN force moved on the evening of 28 December to clear the road blocks and the positions from which it was still being fired on. Once it moved, most of the Tshombist troops fled, as did Tshombe. By 30 December the areas around Elisabethville had been cleared with very little resistance, and Kipushi (the mercenaries' favourite tom-tiddler's-ground on the Rhodesian border) occupied with none at all. Next day a

UN column set off for Jadotville, where it was enthusiasti-
cally welcomed on 3 January; the mercenaries had made
three successive stands at river crossings along the road, but
then fled from the town without pausing to do more than a
fraction of the destruction they had threatened. The mer-
cenary-manned 'Katanga air force' was wiped out in the
first two days of action. UN aircraft were not used against
other targets, and dropped no bombs at all.

The hollowness of Tshombe's threats and boasts that 'his
people' would fight the UN to the death was exposed. There
was no response to his wild appeals for a scorched-earth
resistance by general destruction. After oscillating for three
weeks between Rhodesia and Kolwezi – where many of the
mercenaries had concentrated, threatening to blow up its
big power plant if the UN did not back down – Tshombe
announced that he was abandoning secession and willing to
help carry out the U Thant plan, returned to Elisabethville,
and cooperated in the UN's peaceful occupation of Kolwezi.
The last 400-odd mercenaries fled, mostly into Portuguese-
held Angola, without carrying out their threats to the power
plant. Possibly the end was slightly hastened when Britain
announced that it would no longer approve of the Tshombists' use of Rhodesian soil as a line of communication and
base area – an announcement that came only when the last
embers of the Tshombe régime were already fast cooling.

By mid-1963 the UN force in the Congo had been reduced
by over half, and Thant had declared his aim of withdrawing it altogether by the end of the year. By then, despite
some indications that at least a few of the wilder Katanga
Europeans still hoped, and maybe planned, to restore something like the Tshombe set-up, the reintegration of the
Katanga into the Congo Republic had made considerable
progress, and without the bloodshed that the UN's antagonists had rather gloatingly prophesied. Tshombe himself
was urged, in spite of everything, to cooperate in smoothing
the new path, as many of his former colleagues did; but in
May 1963 he left, via Rhodesia, for Europe – leaving in his

wake his usual trail of contradictory statements, including promises that he would return.

Although much still depended on how stable the Congo government would show itself, the likelihood of any fresh bid to revive the Tshombist régime had been further reduced in 1963 by a significant change of context. In Northern Rhodesia, which in Welensky's heyday had been invaluable to the Tshombist mercenaries and manipulators as a haven, a backstop, and a supply channel, Kenneth Kaunda's African nationalist party had shown its strength in the December 1962 elections and had won a position of power. The white-dominated Rhodesian federation itself was due to be wound up by the end of 1963. Southern Rhodesia remained under white rule, but once federation was finished Welensky would no longer be able to send troops and aircraft from Salisbury up to the Congo border. Portuguese Angola would be the only white-ruled territory bordering on the Katanga; and the Portuguese were having their own troubles.

Nothing, in the turbulent atmosphere of southern Africa, was wholly predictable; but at least it could be recorded that the UN had broken the perilous deadlock caused by the Tshombe secession, had given the newborn Congo a chance to survive infancy, and had fulfilled its duty – expounded by Hammarskjöld in his 1960 and 1961 reports (see pages 118–19) – to help Africans to 'choose their own way' and to resist 'such outside elements as tried to get or protect a foothold within the country'.

For over a year, from September 1961 to January 1963, the Katanga problem seemed the test most likely to make or break the UN. It led to Lord Home's depiction in December 1961 of 'a crisis of confidence in the UN' in Britain. British ministers returned to this theme at intervals during 1962, a year in which UN attention was increasingly turned to the situation in southern Africa and to the British government's policy in regard to Southern Rhodesia in particular. A section of the London Press came to describe the UN as 'the

deadly enemy of the Commonwealth' – although in fact
two thirds of the UN force in the Congo was contributed by
seven Commonwealth nations. Yet British reactions were
rather muffled when the 'third battle of Katanga' came at
the end of 1962. True, a Foreign Office statement, issued
two days after the UN force moved on 28 December, concentrated on 'the futility of trying to impose a political settlement on the Congo by force', and called for an immediate
halt to the UN military action. But the snow-like melting
away of most of the Tshombist soldiery was already apparent.
Thant, and the vast majority of UN member governments,
remained unmoved by the somewhat oddly timed and selec-
tive appeal from London; and London quickly fell almost
silent, except for the by now slightly ritualized agitation
about 'UN atrocities'.

During 1963 the shutting off of the flow of big money into
the Tshombist propaganda machine produced a notable
evaporation of the propaganda itself. Tshombe himself became virtually an 'unperson' even in newspapers that had
made a habit of treating 'the President's' statements with
respect. British diplomacy rallied resiliently: whereas in
January the British embassy in Leopoldville had been
sacked by Congolese angered at London's support for
Tshombe, by July Lord Home was welcoming the Congo
prime minister to London. But whether the scar left on
British sentiment about the United Nations would heal so
quickly was another matter.

NOTES

The foreign affairs debates in both Houses of Parliament on
17 and 18 October 1961 were the first occasion for exchanges in
Parliament, which had not been sitting during September,
about the Katanga events that month. Several questions were
raised about British pressures on the UN. Ministers' statements,
which made some nice distinctions between, for instance, 'inter-
ference' and 'representations', and which gave no indication

that there had been any threat (page 143) of withdrawal of all British support from the UN operation, are worth quoting at some length for what they did reveal. I have italicized some significant words.

1. Labour M.P.s referred to reports that the then British ambassador in the Congo, Ian Scott, had worked for the removal of Rajeshwar Dayal, Hammarskjöld's special representative there until May 1961. (British and American pressure to oust Dayal was unquestionably strong, both in Leopoldville and in New York. See page 131, and Lash, *Dag Hammarskjöld*, page 256.)

Joseph Godber, Minister of State, Foreign Office, said: 'Of course it is proper for our Ambassador to make representations but certainly not to indulge in propaganda such as the hon. Member suggests.'

Tom Driberg: 'What is the difference?'

Godber: 'There is a very big difference.'

2. Denis Healey, Labour M.P., asked about the British Consul's actions in Elisabethville on 28 August (page 135). Healey said: 'There is all too much excuse for the widespread belief ... that his intervention led directly to the catastrophe of September 13.'

Godber: '... he [Healey] went on to claim that there had been pressure from the Western [sic] Consuls, who had interfered to *prevent further* operations of this nature.... H.M. Government has never made representations *of that sort*. We did not seek in any way to *prevent* this operation going on. ...'

Harold Macmillan, Prime Minister: ' ... an allegation that our Consul had somehow *interfered* with the action – that was absolutely untrue – in regard to the dismissal of the mercenaries. ... We have done *nothing* except to *hope* that this would be a successful operation.'

Edward Heath, Lord Privy Seal: 'The Government was greatly *disturbed* by some aspects of the way the operation [of 28 August] was carried out. ...'

3. Healey also asked whether the UN had agreed that the Belgian Consul should be responsible for removing the mercenaries.

Godber: 'I am not informed on that point. It relates to the

UN and to the Belgian Consul, and I have *no information* about it.'

Macmillan: 'It is true, according to *our* information, that the Belgian Consul was *asked* by the UN to undertake *as far as he could* the removal of them [the mercenaries].'

4. In the Lords, Silkin, a Labour peer, quoted reports that, on and after 28 August, British pressure on Hammarskjöld in New York 'not to go as far as he had intended ... gave courage to Mr Tshombe to resist the UN forces'.

Lansdowne, Under-Secretary, Foreign Office, replied: 'We received conflicting accounts and rumours about the UN action on 28 August ... Sir Patrick Dean ... was instructed to *ask* Mr Hammarskjöld what was the exact scope and purpose of the UN intervention; to *find out* whether force had been used before other means had been exhausted; and to *express* the opinion of H.M. Government that there was no mandate for the removal of essential foreign civilians. ... Sir Patrick Dean saw Mr Hammarskjöld *several times* in the course of the week to *discuss* the position.'

5. Notable, in regard to the events of 13 September and after, is the evidence that the Government set out to put strong pressure on the UN on the basis of information which it knew was dubious, and which it later admitted to have been largely false.

Heath: '... the Government learnt with dismay that fighting had broken out in Katanga between UN forces and the *Africans* of Katanga. Communications had by now been broken off between our Consul in Elisabethville and ourselves. It was therefore difficult to obtain any information direct, but ... from these [Press] reports it appeared that UN forces had *attacked Katanga.* ... H.M. Government used *all their influence* to urge a cease-fire. ...'

Lansdowne: '... Our Ambassador in Leopoldville was therefore instructed to see Mr Hammarskjöld on the evening of 13 September to *inquire* about the scope and purpose of the UN action. On 14 September I left for Leopoldville with instructions to acquaint myself with the facts ... and to *impress* upon Mr Hammarskjöld that H.M. Government were shocked at the outbreak of fighting in the Katanga, and to *urge* upon him the necessity of bringing the fighting to a close. ...

(Lansdowne's account of his talk with Hammarskjöld on 16 September began with his finding the Secretary-General both ready to meet Tshombe and ready to give once more the explanation of the UN action that he had given to Riches three days earlier – pages 140 and 143).

'I said that I had reluctantly formed the impression that there was an insufficient desire among certain of his officers to bring about the cease-fire. They seemed to me to be carrying out a *punitive* war. ... I undertook to prepare for the Secretary-General a document setting out in detail the points that worried me. ... Much that I had to say to Mr Hammarskjöld was *highly critical* of the United Nations' action as I understood it. ... At the end of this meeting, I had formed the impression that many of the apparently more outrageous aspects of the UN action as we had seen them from London were inaccurate or exaggerated.'

*

In the Commons debate, Colonel Sir Tufton Beamish urged that 'its [the UN's] procedures should be reformed on the broad lines which are so well understood in so many Parliaments. ... You would blanch, Mr Speaker, if you had been reading with me the report of the debate that took place in the Security Council. ... Some of what was said was not only violent but slanderous ... insinuations galore were made'.

Earlier in the same debate, A. R. Wise, M.P. for Rugby, had called O'Brien 'a bloodthirsty Dublin corner boy' and said that 'the UN troops showed that they were incapable of battle and incapable of discipline ... their most heroic episodes seem to have been confined to slapping women's faces'. In the Lords, Milverton called the UN action 'thuggery'; Winterton called O'Brien a 'filibustering braggard', and found it incomprehensible that the Prime Minister had described alleged 'outrages' by UN troops as 'unsubstantiated'; and the Duke of Montrose dwelt at length on his firm belief that 'the final thing the African feels that the white man has held back from him has been the white woman'.

7 · *Life with Sally*

'UNTIL the Congo crisis, the servants of the United Nations were the unknown men of post-war diplomacy,' remarked a newspaper in June 1962. 'Friends and experts apart, who'd ever heard of Brian Urquhart or George Ivan Smith until they were attacked in Elisabethville?'

A savage beating up with rifle butts is a price most people would rather not pay for fame. But it is true that the 'unknown men' mostly came into the spotlight only when their service to the UN brings them injury – or death. Even then there is not always much of a stir. Many men temporarily seconded to a UN operation, civilians as well as soldiers and regular staff, have died violently but obscurely. Many more have undergone hardship or violence or long-drawn-out risk of violence. Others' involvement in conflicts of interest has brought upon them the anger of one of the disputing sides, or more than one; this, in some cases, means bloodless wounds – abuse, 'character assassination', the stunting or ending of a career.

Khrushchev's doctrine that there are 'no neutral men'* implies that wholehearted personal service to the UN cause is impossible. Fortunately for Russians as well as other peoples, men and women have been found who are ready to hazard themselves for this cause. Perhaps there is nothing remarkable about their physical courage. Brave people serve many causes, good and bad. Nor are the UN's servants unique in being required at times to show patience under provocation, coolness in the face of mob anger, judicial impartiality when some atrocious act stirs their natural emotions. Good policemen, indeed good citizens, may have to show the same qualities. But the UN man in a nasty situation does have to answer for himself two nagging

* Interview with Walter Lippmann, *New York Herald Tribune*, 17 April 1961.

questions: 'What am I sticking my neck out *for*?' and 'Why me?'

For the disciplined professional soldier, these may not be troublesome questions. Whether he volunteered for UN service, or found his unit ordered to it, he may be glad of an active interlude in a dull peacetime career; and danger is part of his trade. But for the civilian it is different. He is neither under military discipline, nor armed or trained to defend himself. He is not flanked by his own compatriots but by an assorted bunch of colleagues, probably with assorted political views, who may differ about just how their joint mission should be conducted; these differences may be easily smoothed out when there is time to talk, but what if violence suddenly erupts and he must at once decide whether duty requires him to place himself – or a colleague – in jeopardy?

It is all very different from the position, say, of a civilian under wartime bombing, with the fate of his own family and neighbours, indeed of his country, at stake. And the UN cannot ensure that its staff at danger points is made up exclusively of heroes; the heroic type, in fact, is not always suitable in an explosive situation.

Today, any reference to UN men in danger areas naturally suggests the Congo. It is worth recalling that this story goes back to 1948. Early in that year a small corps of UN observers, soldiers and civilians drawn from America, Brazil, Britain, China, France, Mexico, and the Netherlands, was deployed in Greece's war-torn border zones. James Douglas, a Secretariat official who served with them, later recalled a small and typical episode, an early-morning arrival with a British officer at a frontier village:

As we toiled up the mountain path to the cluster of houses, we were well aware that a group of villagers in the rocks had their rifles trained on us. 'United Nations' we shouted in Greek as we neared them, and the tension eased.

'You have come in good time', said the village president. 'Our village was raided by guerrillas during the night, and they may return at any moment'. I had to smile when I thought of what two unarmed men could do to protect the village....*

Before the outbreak of the Korean war in 1950, about a thousand men had already seen this kind of UN service, in Greece, Indonesia, Kashmir, Palestine, and Korea itself – where a group of military observers, arriving only a few weeks before the invasion of the south, completed a fortnight's inspection of the partition line just in time to send a report which demolished the Communist claim that the southern forces had started the war. There was risk in all these missions, and the UN's 'men in the field' suffered casualties on several of them, without having any sort of fighting role themselves. Their main job was the essential one of finding out what was really happening behind a fog of conflicting assertions. Their presence also often inhibited acts of violence and aggression, which would have been more extensive if the perpetrators had been sure that there were no authoritative eye-witnesses.

The killing of Folke Bernadotte, the UN Mediator in Palestine, in September 1948, made the world aware of the risks run by the organization's servants in 'front line' areas. He was not alone on its Palestine casualty list. Several lives were lost among the military observers, drawn in the early days from America, Belgium, and France, and the volunteers from the Secretariat and UN headquarters guards who, usually unarmed, served as drivers and escorts. The first of these latter to die by a sniper's bullet was a young Norwegian, Ole Helge Bakke. 'No danger', wrote Trygve Lie later, 'ever deflected UN observers from carrying out their duties.'

The lengthy life of the 5,000-man UN Emergency Force (UNEF) on the Egypt–Israel border has for the most part been a mercifully quiet one. Lurking minefields caused casualties in the early days, but since then the challenge to UNEF has mainly been one of tedium rather than tension. A lot of patience and ingenuity has been put into keeping up morale and preventing friction in a mixed force – Scandi-

* *United Nations News*, July 1956.

navian, Indian, Yugoslav, Canadian, Latin-American –
most of it tied down on repetitive routine duties in a trying
climate a long way from home.

As impressive as the good discipline and good fellowship
of this polyglot army in the hot sand is the fact that it is
still there, having lost its 'emergency' long ago. The governments that agreed to send troops, in the hectic days of 1956,
expected to get them back soon, and two contingents were
in fact withdrawn in 1957; but, despite the failure by
Russia and others to pay their share of the costs, UNEF has
proved an exception to the rule that any international effort
flags as soon as the first panic is over.*

When that panic was on, in November 1956, twenty-four
states offered troops for UNEF within a few days of the idea
being first mooted. Their offers were subject to the terms
that the Assembly approved at the prompting of Hammarskjöld and Pearson, which made clear that UNEF would not
be thrust into combat with anybody, nor be given any task
beyond easing the British, French, and Israeli troops out of
Egypt and helping to avert fresh conflicts. On these terms,
soldiers from many states were available. But at once the
question arose: which of them were *usable*?

This question arises each time a UN presence 'in the
field' is contemplated, be it one civilian or 10,000 soldiers.
Like patriotism in another context, readiness to hazard oneself for the UN cause is not enough. Nor is technical or other
competence. Political eligibility is vital; which means, first
of all, acceptable nationality.

For UNEF, troops from great powers were ineligible from
the start. The UN wanted to get the British and French out,
not to put its sky-blue helmets on them and let them stay in
Egypt. It wanted to keep out the Russians, who seemed all

* Britain, incidentally, provided the largest number of men in the
international force of 3,300 which, under the League of Nations, 'held
the ring' at a time of tension – in the Saar, before and during the 1935
plebiscite. The other troops were Italian, Dutch, and Swedish. But the
Saar force was long in preparation and short in life, in both respects
contrasting with UNEF and the UN Congo force.

too eager to rush in 'volunteers'. So it could not use American troops either, though it gratefully took vital American help in air transport and supply.

Tongues well in cheek, Czechoslovakia and Rumania offered troops, though the Soviet bloc had held aloof from the whole UNEF idea in the 'illegal' emergency Assembly; they were not accepted, and nor were those offered by New Zealand (which had backed Britain in the Assembly) and Pakistan (with which Egypt had been feuding over the Baghdad pact). Hammarskjöld had worked from the start of the UNEF project with Pearson of Canada, Engen of Norway, Francisco Urrutia of Colombia, and Arthur Lall of India, and had early offers from all their countries and, largely through Engen, from the other Scandinavian states too. He and Bunche accepted a few more that they thought should be non-controversial – Brazil, Indonesia, Yugoslavia – and set the others aside as tactfully as they could. Bunche, working a nineteen-hour day, had to find time to pacify, with his characteristic mild ruefulness, indignant delegates who wanted to know what was wrong with their offerings.*

Canada, originator of UNEF, got into the worst trouble. The Egyptians firmly (though politely) argued that Canadians resembled the British too closely for comfort. Deadlock was very near; but the Canadians broke through, at the price of a loud political rumpus at home, by agreeing to send signallers and specialists instead of infantry. Later, when nerves were steadier all round, they contributed an invaluable armoured unit. But Canada's experience has continued to point up the problem of eligibility.

More faithful than most to the honourable idea that readiness to back the UN should be expressed in deeds as well as words, Canada has for years kept an infantry battalion ready for UN service at short notice – and fully inoculated against tropical diseases. But in 1960, when the Congo force was rushed into existence, Canada was begged to send technicians again. As Belgium's ally in NATO, it was

* William R. Frye, *A United Nations Peace Force*, Stevens, London, and Oceana, New York, 1957, gives a vivid account of these days.

again ineligible as a provider of combat troops. However, its signals units, being bilingual in English and French, played a crucial part in the Congo – and in 1963 its airmen were also serving the UN in Yemen.

The intention in the case of the Congo force was that the job must primarily be done by the African states. In a sense, it was a challenge to these states, themselves mostly newly independent, to show that they could help their newest sovereign neighbour out of its travail and refute the argument that Africa could not handle its own affairs. At first they provided about 13,000 of the combat troops, the remaining 2,000 coming from two European countries, Ireland and Sweden, that had no 'bloc' alignments. But the African preponderance was later weakened by the withdrawal of Tunisia's troops (needed at home for the Bizerta conflict with France in 1961); of Sudan's (after Congolese troops had attacked it at the port of Matadi); and of Morocco's, Ghana's, and others when these states took Antoine Gizenga's part in the Congolese political rifts.

Tunisian and Ghanaian units later returned to the force, which was also reinforced by Nigeria and Sierra Leone; but by mid 1962 less than half of its 14,000 combat troops were African, and almost as many were Asian – Indian and Malayan.* India's contribution, made when the force had been gravely weakened by African withdrawals, was of vital significance; and India had made it in the face of harsh criticism, from both the Communist powers and some Europeans (each of these factions being joined by some Africans).

Command in the Congo was as delicate a problem of eligibility as the composition of the force. When the force was formed at lightning speed in July 1960 (the first units actually reaching Leopoldville thirty-six hours after the

* Troops: India 4,615, Malaya 1,613; Ethiopia 2,917, Nigeria 1,691, Tunisia 1,047, Ghana 651, Liberia 238, Sierra Leone 110; Ireland 699, Sweden 663. Other personnel (air, administrative, staff): India 1,093, Pakistan 683, Canada 317, Sweden 273, Norway 137, others 322.

first Council resolution), the UN was fortunately able to find
a commander immediately, as in 1956, in the person of the
Chief of Staff of its Truce Supervision Organization (UNTSO)
in Jerusalem. Carl von Horn, the Swedish general who then
held Burns's old post, was eligible enough (although
President Nkrumah of Ghana intermittently pressed for an
all-African command); and he was provided with African
deputies. This did not prevent the Russians, once they broke
with the UN operation, from branding the Congo command
as 'colonialist'. Hammarskjöld's retort was that

> this United Nations Command, which is now said to represent
> a colonizing element, apart from the Supreme Commander,
> who is from a country which never had any colonies, consists of
> one Moroccan and one Ethiopian general, at present assisted by
> an Indian general. ... I begin to feel uncertain what this word
> (colonizers) means. ...

The Russians went on hammering away. In November 1961
in the Council, Zorin, addressing himself to the Americans,
said:

> You had your machinery there (in the Congo) ... you had
> your troops of the United Nations there ... you had a high
> command of the UN acting on your instructions, under your
> orders. ...

Throughout 1961 the Commander had in fact been
General Sean McKeown, of Ireland, again with African and
Indian deputies; in April 1962 General Kebede Gebre, of
Ethiopia, succeeded him and held the post until mid 1963.

The Russian's major target was the UN's civilian chain of
command in the Congo, rather than the military one. Here,
their aim of arousing Afro-Asian suspicion of Hammarskjöld was made easier by the fact that he relied heavily, in
the early stages, on two or three Americans. He had sent out
Ralph Bunche, the UN's veteran trouble-shooter, even before
the Congo's independence day, to start setting up the
extensive UN aid which he foresaw the new state would need.
When the storm broke, Bunche stayed on as the head of the
UN operation, struggling with every kind of chaos –

including irruptions of wild mutineers into his hotel room in the middle of the night. Within a few weeks the Communists were pouncing on his American nationality to discredit the UN in African eyes – while ignoring his Negro race.

The charge that he was taking orders from Washington was utterly unfounded; but the rule that 'loyalty to the UN is not enough' operated – Bunche's vulnerability as an American weakened the UN's hand. Hammarskjöld asked India for the loan of Rajeshwar Dayal, an experienced diplomat who had already done the UN good service in Lebanon in 1958. Nehru agreed, but reluctantly, as Dayal was doing vital work as India's high commissioner in Pakistan (with which India's relations were then at a promising but very delicate state). To hold the fort between the battered Bunche's departure and Dayal's arrival, Hammarskjöld sent out his own Executive Assistant, Andrew Cordier – who, as a Secretariat veteran since 1946, as Hammarskjöld's close confidant and virtual deputy, and as a key man in the Congo operation from the start, could take over without needing time to study the situation.

But Cordier was another American; and the showdown between Kasavubu and Lumumba in early September 1960 came while he was in charge. He stuck to Hammarskjöld's ruling that the UN must not prejudge the constitutional dispute by recognizing either of the disputing factions; but, faced suddenly with the threat of civil war in Leopoldville itself, where Lumumba was broadcasting fiery appeals to his supporters to come out and fight, he ordered the closing of the local radio station and the halting of movements of non-UN soldiery by air.

A non-Western UN representative in the Congo might well have seen no alternative but to do precisely the same; a full-scale armed clash between the factions in the capital could have produced a disaster with which the UN could not possibly cope. But the fact that it was an American UN official who took the decision strengthened the case against Hammarskjöld which Russia had already begun to build up.

In the Council on 9 September, Hammarskjöld fully

endorsed Cordier's action (there had been no time to consult him about it), and commented that this was 'a situation which it is easy to sit in New York and discuss in terms of protocol, but which it requires wisdom and courage to handle when you are at the front'. Considering that the UN action, however impartial in form and aim, proved a severe check to Lumumba, what was notable at this stage was the refusal of the Afro-Asians to follow Russia in assailing the Secretariat. Thus Alex Quaison-Sackey of Ghana, in the Council on 16 September, criticized the closing of the radio and airports in restrained words, and had both Zorin and Hammarskjöld flushing a bright red when he brought in a quotation from Edmund Burke:

My President would like me to appeal to the Council to refrain from all personal attacks on Mr Hammarskjöld. The clear vision of this man, 'his merited rank, his superior eloquence, his splendid qualities, his eminent services, the vast place he fills in the eyes of mankind' must embolden us to pay tribute to him for his great services in the cause of peace.

And Nkrumah himself, in the Assembly on 23 September, while complaining specifically that the UN had used Ghanaian troops to shut down the radio, said that 'it would be entirely wrong to blame either the Security Council or any senior officials of the UN for what has taken place'.

At later stages in the Congo operation, Hammarskjöld took more pains to blunt the Soviet charges by spreading responsibility among the Afro-Asians. He made greater use of the advisory committee of delegates that he had formed in August 1960, which represented the states contributing troops to the Congo force, and was thus mainly Afro-Asian. More significant still was the evolution of the 'Congo Club', the group of Secretariat men who worked most closely with him on the operation.

Cordier, Bunche, and Heinz Wieschhoff* – all three of

---

* Wieschhoff, German by origin and an anthropologist by training, was an 'old Africa hand', long on the UN's Trusteeship staff, and later secretary of the Assembly's political committee. Hammarskjöld called him his *éminence grise* in African affairs; they died together at Ndola.

them American – had been founder members. Sir Alexander MacFarquhar, a former Indian Civil Servant, was brought in to handle civilian operations at the New York end, and General Rikhye of India, a UNEF veteran, as chief military adviser there. Chakravarti Narasimhan, another Indian, who, like Bunche, was serving as an Under-Secretary for Special Political Affairs – that is, as a senior official 'without portfolio', available for special assignments – joined the club, and took on a central role when in mid 1961 he replaced Cordier (who later retired).

By then the club also embraced several Africans, although their assignments in the field made them 'country members' at times. Taieb Sahbani of Tunisia spent months in 1961 as UN representative in Brussels, trying to modify the Belgian attitude to the Katanga secession. Francis Nwokedi of Nigeria and Robert Gardiner of Ghana served as special UN emissaries in the Congo itself, particularly in the struggle to reconcile the political factions and restore parliamentary legitimacy. (Gardiner later served as officer in charge of the whole Congo operation in 1962.)

This trend aroused fears in some western quarters that were almost a mirror image of the Soviet complaints of western dominance in the Secretariat. The way Dayal was ousted under American and British pressure has already been mentioned (page 131). Some western comment on Narasimhan's succession to Cordier's post showed less concern about the undoubted loss of experience involved in Cordier's departure after fifteen years, than about the prospect of a key post being 'lost to the West'. At bottom, it seems, many westerners agree with Khrushchev that there are 'no neutral men' – the proposition on which the Soviet demand for a 'troika' was based.

There is no questioning the fact that the Secretariat was unbalanced in national composition at the start. Two thirds of the original staff were American, British, or French. Recruiting had to be done quickly, and these were the nationalities most immediately available in 1946. The unbalance has been progressively reduced (with the inevitable

result that citizens of countries originally over-represented
have had relatively poor prospects of getting in). Up to
1961, however, the basic formula was to recruit staff
roughly in proportion to their countries' shares of the UN
budget. America, Britain, and France were down to 600
posts out of a total professional staff of 1,400, but North
America and Western Europe as a whole accounted for
over 850. An expert committee then proposed a new formula that takes into account populations as well as budget
contributions. This found general acceptance, though the
practical application took time to work out.

The new formula would apparently leave virtually unchanged the quotas of America, Australia, many Latin-
American and Asian and some smaller European states. It
would increase the quotas of Asia and Africa as a whole,
while cutting the numbers of posts now held by citizens of
some of them, in particular India, Ceylon, Egypt, and
Ghana; and it would cut down quite sharply the British,
French, Dutch, and Belgian numbers. It would not give the
Communist states larger quotas than they have already
been entitled to (their man on the committee demanded
one third of all posts, on 'troika' lines). But these states' past
record (except for Poland) had been one of continuous
failure to offer candidates to fill the professional posts – over
200 – to which they were entitled. What was significant
after 1961 was that they looked like making more real effort
actually to provide officials – though they were still reluctant
to let them stay with the UN for long.

Russia, indeed, actually urged that the entire Secretariat should consist of short-service staff. This would put
paid to the idea of a real international loyalty, and throw
things right back to the days before Drummond gave the
League a staff that – against all precedent – was not just a
jumble of national officials on short loan. Hitherto only a
fifth of the Secretariat have been short-service men, of whom
a good many are specially qualified people deliberately
taken on for specific temporary jobs; but the majority of
the Soviet bloc officials serve for only a year or two, being

called home when they have learnt enough about the UN
(and the outside world at large) to be valuable to their
government, but before they have been tempted to open
their dutifully closed minds too far, or to catch the infection
of loyalty to the UN.

Even the presumed Soviet 'trusties' who have successively
held a senior post as assistant secretary-general or under-
secretary, usually in charge of Security Council affairs, have
averaged only two to three years. Seven Russians followed
one another in the top echelon in the first eighteen years.*
Their conduct has been 'correct', with a few lapses;
notably by Arkadyev, who in December 1960 went off one
night to a Soviet delegation party without telling Hammarskjöld that Zorin had initiated an urgent Council meeting
for the next day – and who resigned soon after a Council
session, in January 1962, during which he passed Zorin five
notes evidently advising him how to challenge the chairman
on points of order.

But it has been a recurring problem for each Secretary-
General how to handle delicate diplomatic business when
one of his chief political officials is a man who is – as a
shrewd colleague said of Sobolev – 'a first-class administrator, but not working for this Organization'. In most
cases where a really sensitive matter was involved, the
solution was simply to bypass the Soviet under-secretary.
In 1950, Lie formed a 'Korea Club' of senior officials,
excluding Zinchenko; and Alfred Katzin, Lie's liaison man
for Korea, worked directly to Lie and Cordier. In 1960,
Arkadyev was similarly bypassed, although Wieschhoff, a
key Congo man, was technically his deputy.

The problem is older than the UN, and not exclusively a
Soviet one. In the League Secretariat, officials drawn from
Fascist Italy developed a manner of acting as if they were
part of their own country's bureaucracy, not of the League's.

---

* Arkady Sobolev (later a deputy foreign minister) to 1949;
Constantin Zinchenko to 1953; Ilya Chernyshev to 1957; Anatoli
Dobrynin (later ambassador in Washington) to 1960; Georgy Arkadyev
to 1962; Evgeny Kiselev to 1963; and Vladimir Suslov, from May 1963.

And while Italy and Germany were still League members, their representatives on a committee that reviewed the work of the Secretariat urged – unsuccessfully – that the aim of international loyalty should be discarded, and that the Secretariat's political work should be guided by a group of senior officials who would openly represent their respective countries.

At San Francisco in 1945, Russia proposed that the UN Secretary-General should serve for only two years and should not be eligible for re-election; that four deputies should be similarly elected (the veto applying to all these elections); and that all five men should be nationals of the Big Five. At first the other four of the Big Five went most of the way with Russia. But the smaller states resisted stoutly. Canada said the plan meant 'the practical domination of the Secretariat by the great powers'. New Zealand warned that it 'would produce a crisis in the Secretariat at the beginning of its work'.

The mice won this round against the lions. The great-power plan was completely rejected. The Charter left the Secretary-General free to appoint his staff himself, subject to whatever regulations the Assembly (that is, the mice) laid down, and to due regard to recruiting 'on as wide a geographical basis as possible' (which, however, was to take second place to efficiency and integrity). Thus, whatever other privileges the founders assigned to the great powers, they made it very plain that no built-in position for them was to be established in the Secretariat.

In practice, the Secretary-General's choice of top staff is circumscribed both by political pressures and by the availability of suitable men. Lie was firmly told by the great powers that each of them must have a man in the top bracket; but, although he accepted this as a necessity if the UN was to be got off the ground, he did not find them all ready to follow through by offering him high-calibre candidates. Lie's original top echelon, almost inevitably in the conditions of 1946, was heavily European and of variable quality. Although over the years a wholly new row of faces has appeared in the front seats,* and various top posts have been renamed, reshuffled, merged, or divided up, the old problem of combining a politically acceptable distribution of nationalities with the acquiring of the best man for each post is still a problem; and the top echelon has never functioned as a true policy-shaping 'cabinet' (even in the American, far less in the British, sense). The particular complication involving the Soviet under-secretary has not been the only reason for this.

Three questions are, in fact, involved here, all of them bearing directly on the disputed nature of the Secretariat: How far should states be allowed to press claims for influential posts in it? How should the Secretary-General be equipped with advisers? and: How should he be equipped with men whom he can confidently use as his representatives on delicate political missions?

Obviously some compromise has to be struck between these requirements. But it is also obvious that the compromise must be weighted in favour of the third requirement, if the Secretariat is to cope with its developing role. The jealousies of states have to be allowed for to a certain extent; because, the more unbalanced the composition of the Secretariat, the more vulnerable it is to charges of prejudice. Again, although the Secretary-General can get most of the guidance he needs about member states' attitudes directly from their own diplomats at the UN, he can probably learn more, if only about national psychologies, by surrounding himself with a widely representative senior staff. But his crucial need is for usable men: men whom he can entrust with tasks as complex as the Congo operations – which means men inbued as far as possible with his own interpretation of the UN consensus, *and* of eligible nationality.

One of Hammarskjöld's early innovations was to appoint two under-secretaries 'without portfolio', free from full-time departmental duties. Bunche was, and remains, one; as

* David Owen (British) and Victor Hoo (Chinese), two of Lie's earliest top men, were still in UN service in 1963, but both had moved into technical assistance work.

such, he has been in the thick of most UN 'crisis' jobs for years – but not all of them, and that is the point. In the 1958 Lebanon–Jordan crisis, for instance, Bunche was not usable as a special emissary, because his own country, America, was too directly involved. Nor, for the same reason, was Sir Humphrey Trevelyan, the very able British diplomat whom Hammarskjöld had just acquired as his other 'without portfolio' man (and on whom, he had said privately, he was counting for some sharp-edged new ideas to replace the old ones that he and Bunche had been batting to and fro too long). But in 1958 the UN was largely preoccupied with Middle Eastern issues in which even a Briton with Trevelyan's good repute among the Arabs could not be used to much purpose. By the end of the year, tired of thumb-twiddling, he had left.

Earlier, Hammarskjöld had tried out his top Soviet man at the time, Chernyshev, as an under-secretary without portfolio – with minimal results. Thant at first paired Bunche in the 'Special Political Affairs' bracket with his newly acquired Egyptian under-secretary, Omar Loutfi; when Loutfi died in 1963, 'Dragon' Protitch, a Yugoslav veteran with wide UN experience, succeeded him.

A quick thought may suggest that all the UN needs to do is to stock up with senior men from non-aligned countries, whom neither America nor Russia can denounce as the other's agent. (Indonesia, in 1961, actually suggested that all under-secretaries should be drawn from these countries.) However, the actual structure of the world is less simple than the crude mock-up used for Khrushchev's 'troika'. An Egyptian, for instance, would not be usable for UN purposes in regard to either an Arab–Israel or an inter-Arab dispute; whereas the Canadian Burns and the Italian Spinelli, both 'aligned', were acceptable as chief of UNEF and as UN 'presence' in Jordan. Another example: Ellsworth Bunker, the retired American ambassador who in 1962, under Thant's auspices, helped to coax Indonesia and the Netherlands into agreement on West New Guinea (Irian), was a more acceptable 'good offices' man in this case than a citizen of an Afro-Asian 'uncommitted' country, whom the Dutch might have seen as committed on Indonesia's side.

Even citizens of ex-imperial countries have sometimes served the UN on missions where anti-colonial feeling was intensely involved, without incurring criticism except in the ex-imperial countries themselves: Urquhart and Michel Tombelaine, a Frenchman whose UN loyalty made him the target of particularly violent menaces from French and Belgian *'ultras'* in the Katanga, are instances.

Yet the need for usable men suggests that a high proportion of senior UN staff should be drawn from countries not too closely identified with great-power interests; and if, as has been shown, even a non-aligned national is often disqualified in a particular case, this may merely indicate that the UN should have a wider range of non-aligned men to choose from. What a Secretary-General does not need, and should be saved from, is a top echelon that has been shaped (or thinks it has been shaped) as a 'cabinet' representing member states' interests.

The place for a UN 'cabinet' of that kind is outside the Secretariat, among the diplomats who are openly and quite properly representing their governments – not inside, where international loyalty has been slowly and painfully becoming a reality, however short of perfection it still falls. On the outside, if the Security Council cannot be reformed and made to fill the bill, something might yet be done on the basis of the Assembly's General Committee, which is now more balanced in representation than the Council but too large to be fully efficient.* Each appointment by the Assembly of a 'select committee' of its own members for a

* The General Committee began with fourteen members, but by the end of 1963 had twenty-five. In debate on a proposal to enlarge it to twenty-one in 1957, a British delegate gave warning that Parkinson's law on the expansion of committees showed that twenty-one was the point of growth at which any such body began to 'perish'; from then on, the real work would be done by some smaller cabal, while the full committee listened to speeches. Nobody contested the point, but the increase to twenty-one was inevitably approved the next day. Parkinson's laws are remorseless.

specific purpose is a move in this direction; but more needs to be done to fill the gap that yawns too often between the cumbrous Assembly and the lonely Secretary-General, too often left without clear guidance.

Attempts to enmesh him in a spider's web of 'representative' top officials are quite another thing, and could, if successful, destroy the Secretariat's ability to act effectively. This applies not only to Khrushchev's troika demand, but also to other demands that were voiced before U Thant's election in November 1961. The Russians were not alone in trying to lay down in advance how Thant's top men should be picked and how he should be required to consult them. Some Asians and Africans inclined toward a veiled form of 'sub-troika'; and a caucus meeting of West European delegations produced a statement insisting that Europe must have 'its rightful place' in the Secretariat's top rank. Fortunately Thant, with skill and some help, was able to escape from the meshes. He did not commit himself to act always on the advice of his chief political assistants; or to consult all of them when facing a decision; or even to retain their services. He was thus left free to do, and later did, a number of things that inevitably displeased various interested states, but which he deemed essential.

If the Secretariat could never do such things, the UN would be without an executive. (Any idea that the Council is an 'executive' is a myth; even as a deliberative body, it has often proved slower than the Assembly to agree on an urgently needed authorizing resolution.) And one must here restate the plain fact that the executive is bound to go on giving offence to some from time to time, even though it is acting within the terms of a general UN consensus. 'You can't win.' The Secretariat will displease some elements, whether or not what it does (or refrains from doing) turns out in the light of history to have been the wisest choice. Nor will it always turn out to have been right. Archangels are not available for UN service; the choice is between an executive manned by human beings capable of misjudgement, and none at all.

The UN can boob, and does. One of the worst boobs occurred in 1962, in the shape of the astonishing affair of the mission led by a Filipino delegate, Victorio Carpio, which visited South-West Africa and returned trailing inglorious clouds of contradiction, recrimination, and excuse. The Secretariat can get little comfort from the fact that its own record shows nothing to match the more squalid acts of some of its masters – the governments and their delegations. Any mud that is going splashes over the UN as a whole.

People who live in the 'big glasshouse' can't usually throw stones, or mud, back. As most of the Secretariat's work is, by its nature, distinctly non-profit-making and short on tangible results, it is a sitting target for charges that it is mostly made up of overpaid layabouts. These charges are hardly fair to the contributing governments' financial experts, who rightly and regularly scrutinize the accounts, and whose main headache is not a Secretariat passion for sinecurism, but the habit among the governments themselves of ordering the staff to undertake new tasks while declining to furnish the necessary funds. Criticism of rates of pay, whether emanating from the *Express* newspapers or from *Izvestia,* usually shows ignorance (sometimes studied) of cost-of-living levels in New York and other places where UN officials have to serve, as well as of the UN's need to offer inducements that enable it to compete for talent with rival employers.

The work load is, certainly, often distributed unevenly. Both at headquarters and in the field, it is a recurring experience to find some officials labouring mightily and others merely ticking over. There are, however, two reasons for this which are virtually inherent in the organization. One is the arbitrary nature of special calls on the UN. There are limits to the extent to which loads like the Congo can be spread over the whole staff. The other is that old friend, 'equitable geographical distribution'.

The UN is not bound to keep half a dozen complete duds from Anonymia on its payroll for all time just to satisfy

Anonymian pride. But it is morally bound to give a few reasonably promising Anonymians a chance to show their worth. And it frankly accepts a role as something of a training school for officials from small new nations; reasoning – justifiably – that it is part of the UN's job to help these states train their officials, and that it is in the UN's interest that they should acquire a nucleus of people who have experienced international teamwork and know what the UN is about.

It would be splendid, of course (though not very comfortable), if the entire staff were visibly dedicated to the cause. People being people, especially in bureaucracies, not very many of them are. (It would be invidious to name here some individuals who are undoubtedly dedicated, and embarrassing to those of them who like to conceal the fact behind an irreverent manner.) What can be said is that the Secretariat itself is wryly aware that the pure flame of idealism seldom shines so pure through years of departmental duty. In its house organ, *Secretariat News,* an anonymous wit once offered, under the heading 'Ten years in the life of an international Civil Servant', two letters written by the same fictitious character:

To the Personnel Department.   27 March 1951
Dear Sir,

... I have always dreamed of being able to make the world a better place in which to live. ... I respectfully request that I be considered for a position with the Secretariat. ... My starting salary is unimportant. I ask merely for the chance to serve in some capacity through which I can aid my fellow man. ...

To the Office of the Controller.   27 March 1961
Dear Harry,

In checking my pay statement this month, I noticed that I received only $1,027·63 whereas, according to my calculations, I should have received $1,027·98. Could you please look into the matter? ... I must protest the high-handed manner in which you disallowed my claim for $550 per diem, covering the four days I spent in Bombay.... An international Civil

Servant should travel in accommodations commensurate with his dignity.

Not all of them saints, not all heroes, and some of them anything but, the UN's servants have yet produced, almost by chance, from their motley ranks an essential quota of people willing to take risks in attempting a task which (and this is the point) there is nobody better, indeed usually nobody else, to do. The underlying question is not whether they do it perfectly – they don't – but what would happen if they were not prepared to do it at all. Trouble may be their business; but few people, in the Secretariat or anywhere else, go all the way in readiness to meet it with Urquhart, who, shortly after being half killed in Katanga, with a sincerity as indisputable as his cracked ribs, said he was 'delighted if, when I'm in one of these jobs, people start attacking me rather than attacking one another'.*

'No policeman can be universally popular,' said President Kennedy, in his 1962 message on the State of the Union appealing to Americans to support the UN whatever dissent there might be from each of its particular decisions or actions. Urquhart, in *The Times* of 30 April 1962, spelt some of this out with a cheerfully dry touch:

Ingenious journalists see all the faults without registering the problems, and can, and do, point out deceptively direct and simple solutions, which have not, of course, been adopted.

If positive action is taken, it is partisan and interfering. If action is deferred, it shows lack of decisiveness or a failure to carry out the mandate. All of this makes the international official's job interesting and full of incentive. . . .

U Thant, speaking in London in July 1962 about the Congo operation, made sober reference to the loss of lives and the accusations and indignities that it had brought upon

* Interview in the *Sunday Times*, 4 March 1962. As Kenneth Pickthorn, M.P., has written to *The Times* rather tartly about 'the new oligarchy of people in Britain who know Brian Urquhart and George Ivan Smith', I had better declare my interest and confess (although no oligarch) to knowing them and, what may be worse, liking them.

the organization's servants, affirming that 'the United Nations must inevitably accept the risks and insults involved'. Lightening his philosophy, he added:

One of the most important roles of the United Nations ... is that of the old English institution, Aunt Sally – the large and conspicuous figure at which things can be thrown both with impunity and with almost complete certainty of hitting the target. ...

Life with Aunt Sally is not always easy. Some of the campaigns mounted against UN officials have aimed at making it intolerable, for both the individual victim and the executive as a whole. Without believing in 'the United Nations, right or wrong', one can still grasp the fact that, if many such campaigns succeed, the growth of a UN executive role will be stunted.

8 · *Forward Look*

A FEW weeks before he died, Hammarskjöld warned the United Nations that, in effect, if it did not go forward it would go back – back to anarchy, if not to Armageddon.

The events of 1960–1, he pointed out in the introduction to his annual report, had shown that the member states must choose between two quite different concepts of the UN's character. Some saw it strictly as 'a static conference machinery' – a concept 'firmly anchored in the time-honoured philosophy of sovereign national states in armed competition'. Others saw it as 'a dynamic instrument' through which executive action might be taken to resolve conflicts and, where possible, to forestall them. This dynamic concept took the traditional notion of a diplo-matic conference only as a starting-point, 'envisaging the possibility of continued growth'.

He showed, point by point, how the dynamic concept fitted both the letter and the spirit of the Charter; how the static conference concept fitted neither. Those who pre-ferred the conference concept, he said, would naturally tend to 'side-step the mandatory nature' of Council decisions; to oppose 'a gradual increase in the weight of decisions of the Assembly'; to refuse 'to shoulder the financial consequences of a decision'; to ignore the Charter's insistence on the ex-clusively international character of the Secretariat; and to resent the Secretary-General's developing role in cases in which, receiving little or no guidance from Assembly or Council about how to carry out their wishes, he had to 'shoulder responsibility for certain limited political func-tions'.

It was up to the governments to choose. But it was up to him to give warning that

those whose reactions to the work of the Organization hamper its development, or reduce its possibilities of effective action, may have to shoulder the responsibility for a return to a state of affairs which governments had already found too dangerous after the First World War.

This was much more than a defence against Khrushchev's attack. It amounted to an invitation to all member governments to look deeply into their own split minds. The invitation remains as valid as it was in August 1961.

Hammarskjöld made no exaggerated claims, in this 'political testament' or elsewhere, for a dominant role for the UN in resolving the most massive of the world's present problems. He had no illusions that it could order the great powers about. He staked the more modest claim that it should have the 'right to make its voice heard' when peace was imperilled by their jarring together over an issue like Berlin. And by 'its voice', in such a context, he clearly meant the voice of 'the majority of nations who wish to stand aside from the big-power conflicts'.

It was in providing at least some degree of protection for those smaller nations that he felt the UN was already showing a certain effectiveness. He had expressed this feeling a year earlier, when Khrushchev was hammering at him in the Assembly. Russia's troika plan, he then said, would mean that the UN could not 'serve as an effective instrument for active protection of the interests of those many Members who need such protection'.

It is not the Soviet Union, or indeed any other big powers, who need the UN for their protection; it is all the others. In this sense the Organization is first of all *their* Organization.... I shall remain in my post ... as long as they wish me to do so.

His successor, U Thant, echoed this belief when he said, at Uppsala on 6 May 1962:

I am in complete agreement with my distinguished predecessor, Mr Dag Hammarskjöld, when he said that it is the small nations, rather than the great powers, which need the protection the United Nations can give.

Significantly, Thant was more concerned in that speech

with the small nations' duties than with their rights; in particular, with their duty to build bridges between the great powers in order to make possible the strengthening of the UN's authority.

On the shoulders of the smaller nations now rests, undoubtedly, much of the responsibility for the future fate of the United Nations. This can hardly be a happy thought for those who are apt to label small states as inherently irresponsible. Perhaps the fears of such people will be assuaged if they look a little more carefully at the evidence – some of it recorded in this book – of the practical service that has already been given to the UN by small states and their citizens. Small states are not peopled by purer souls than great-power states. Grotesque and alarming antics mark the records of both.* But three things can be said. Not only the Scandinavians, but other small states too, including some of the new nations, have repeatedly made positive contributions to the UN's work. Among others, a greater sense of responsibility may well grow as they become more aware how much now depends on them. Above all, the small states are discovering their own real interest in the effective development of the United Nations.

Rough water lies ahead. The threat of bankruptcy, created by the refusal of Russia, France, the Arabs, and some other members to pay their due shares toward the costly UN peace-keeping operations in the Congo or on the Egypt–Israel border, was only temporarily averted in 1962 by the sale of UN bonds. The International Court in July 1962 gave an opinion that the costs of the Congo and UNEF operations are, like other UN costs, fully subject to the Assembly's authority to assess member governments. But this issue, even if it is pressed to the point of denying the right to vote in the Assembly to those who fall two years behind with

---

* A visitor at the 1960 Assembly, happening to catch Khrushchev in one of his fits of shouting and desk-pounding (while the newly admitted African delegations sat in sober ranks all around him), is said to have asked: 'Which *are* the new nations?'

their dues, may remain unresolved for some time yet. Meanwhile, doubts whether the UN could raise the necessary funds if it became involved in another large-scale operation like the Congo seem bound to have an inhibiting effect. In 1962–3, the UN was able to undertake additional tasks in West Irian (New Guinea), Yemen, and North Borneo because the governments concerned (Indonesia and the Netherlands; Egypt and Saudi Arabia; Indonesia, Malaya, and Philippines) agreed to share the costs themselves. In other cases, however, this may not be possible. And if a 'financial veto' should eventually prove an effective way of hamstringing the UN, the rejoicing will not necessarily be confined to Moscow. The Katanga secessionists' long defiance of the UN was partly sustained by belief that the UN force would have to leave the Congo quite quickly owing to sheer lack of money to keep it there.

The short term of office for which Thant was appointed in November 1961 was to end in April 1963, when Hammarskjöld's second five-year term would have ended. When Thant was sworn in, Zorin declared that Russia had agreed to his appointment only because of the urgent need for a decision; it maintained its demand that the office of Secretary-General should be replaced by a 'troika'. In November 1962 Russia had to back down, and Thant was voted a term extending to 1966. But the battle of the troika may be fought again. The battle for the Chinese seat will certainly be fought again. No two-to-one majority for seating Peking's men is yet in sight (page 75); but if and when their take-over of the Chinese seat comes to appear imminent, a severe strain will be placed on the American administration's ability to give the UN the support which has been of crucial importance to it when, as in the Congo, it has run into trouble with the other great powers.

Much depends on the conjuncture of events. The Chinese Communists, after taking their places in the UN, might well prove a less disastrous new element there than many Americans expect – and awkward partners for Russia (whose tactics in regard to the Chinese seat have shown an interesting ambivalence). But if the struggle over the seat reached a climax while Russia was pressing again for its troika and Britain was still seriously embroiled with the UN over southern Africa, the total strain could be greater than any before.

If the middle powers and smaller states rallied to the UN, as they have good reason to do, it might once again show an unexpected capacity for survival. If so, some accommodation with the two super-powers could eventually be reached. A more darkly troubling prospect has been that of a lasting alienation of the former imperial powers of western Europe, and of Britain in particular, as a result of the struggle for power in southern Africa.

Already this group has found itself repeatedly isolated in the UN. Most of the resolutions on Angola, South African racialism, South West Africa, and colonialism in general were carried in the 1961 and 1962 Assemblies by majorities ranging from ninety to ninety-nine. Belgium, Britain, France, Portugal, South Africa, and Spain appeared in twos and threes as the only contrary voters, sometimes the only abstainers. When the resolution urging Britain to call a conference for constitutional reform in Southern Rhodesia was carried on 24 June 1962 by seventy-three to one, there were twenty-seven abstentions (mainly European and Latin-American countries); but only South Africa voted against, while Britain and Portugal did not take part in the vote.

Calling these resolutions 'reckless and careless of peace', as Home did in 1961, is not going to stop them. British ministers have tried to depict the UN pressure against white rule in southern Africa as the work of a small 'irresponsible' and 'over-vocal' minority. But the plain fact is that it represents a very broad movement of world opinion; and that the widespread respect for Britain's good general record of post-war 'disimperialism' has been matched by an equally widespread suspicion of British intentions in the white-dominated and mineral-rich region stretching south from the Katanga. In the case of Southern Rhodesia, the

British government's twin arguments* – that it could not interfere there, and nor could the UN – merely nurtured a particular suspicion that when, for instance, Home claimed (July 1962) that 'we are trying our hardest to achieve a programme of decolonization', the reality was a programme for insulating the colony's white-run system from the political pressures of Africa as a whole.

The UN did not invent these pressures. It mirrors them. If there were no UN, or if, like the pre-war League, it was an essentially European institution, Africa's 'wind of change' would not be blowing across Turtle Bay; but it would be blowing no less strongly – and most likely with a more bitter edge to it, imparted from the north-east. Moscow and Peking both work hard to convince Africans still struggling against colonial or racial rule that their salvation can come only from the Communist powers.

As it is, one of the UN's most striking characteristics is the extent to which it has frustrated the Communist powers' hopes of directing the Afro-Asian anti-colonial movement. If they could have captured the leadership of that movement, the entire balance of world force would have swung to their advantage. Instead, the development of the UN has provided an alternative focus, and has helped the Africans and Asians to 'choose their own way' – as their repeated spurning of Soviet leads in the Assembly has shown.

Nagging of the colonial powers from the UN can be called irritating. It could also be criticized for having been inadequate. If more pressure had been put on Belgium, at an early stage, to give the Congolese a chance to gain political experience, the catastrophe of 1960 might have been avoided. If more pressure had been put on Portugal, both the bloodshed in Angola and the summary seizure of Goa by India, after fourteen years of deadlock, might have been avoided. Article 73 of the Charter laid upon the

* In October 1962 Sir Hugh Foot resigned from Britain's UN delegation, making it clear that he could no longer support these arguments, and that he feared disaster if there was no change in Rhodesian policy.

colonial powers, 'as a sacred trust', the obligation 'to take due account of the political aspirations of the peoples [of dependencies] and to assist them in the progressive development of their free political institutions'.

That article alone is enough (though there is plenty more in the Charter) to show that the founders did not plan the UN as a means of perpetuating the *status quo*. The intention, on the contrary, was to see that change should take place as peacefully as possible. This must imply, in practice, both 'nagging' – that is, urging that change should begin well before the danger point of explosion is reached; and 'interfering' – that is, when conflict is imminent or actual, introducing some UN entity to moderate the scale of the violence. The alternative to these irritating procedures can be seen in the seven years' war in Algeria, with its staggering casualties, its massive destruction, and its harvest of fear and bitterness and confusion.

Can we look further ahead? Home, in his 1961 Berwick speech, struck one hopeful note when he described colonialism as 'transient', and argued that it would not 'distort the outlook' of UN members for more than 'a few more years'. There are signs and portents here. Not only have an impressive number of the Afro-Asian states already shown that they prefer moderate to extreme formulations on colonial questions, and that they are not so wholly preoccupied with colonialism as to think only superficially about other great world issues. It is also possible that a France disengaged from Algeria and not otherwise at odds with the Afro-Asian world may emerge with unexpected speed from the isolated position it has recently occupied at the UN. Britain, for its part, has already seen fit to modify slightly its former solidarity with Portugal and South Africa in UN voting.

Not for a long time is the UN likely to be done with the preoccupations of the post-colonial age – the conflicts between and within weak and unstable new states which are ever liable to draw in other countries and create a need for the UN to 'intervene in the name of non-intervention'.

But if the West European powers are less directly involved in such situations, their resolution may be an easier matter. At the same time, the experience of working together in the common cause of preventing local troubles from spreading may benefit old and new states alike, fostering mutual trust where there is now suspicion.

If such teamwork promotes trust, the strengthening of the UN will become easier. One particular barrier to its development has hitherto been the fear among newly independent states that UN armed forces might be instruments by which their former masters could regain a hold on them. Given time and growing trust, this fear, which has already diminished, may cease to be an obstacle to the building up of really substantial strength behind the UN's elbow. This has an importance that goes beyond the problem of dealing effectively with local conflicts in the world as we know it today.

The programmes for general disarmament sponsored by both Western and Communist countries, and the principles for disarmament advanced by non-aligned countries too, now all have in common a recognition that disarmament must be matched by the building up of UN capacity for protecting the disarmed. They also have in common a notable vagueness about how this is to be done.

The vagueness is not surprising. After disarmament, whatever authority controlled the UN forces would be invincible. (If it was not invincible, it would be incapable, and disarmament would not last long.) However scrupulously the authority might seek not to use its power to interfere in states' domestic politics, it could not avoid having an often decisive influence on those politics. Even its decisions *not* to act would have their impact. (If Anonymia, genuinely troubled by internal violence, enlarges its domestic security forces above the permitted level, and the authority does nothing to stop it, Ruritania will take note, and may enlarge its own forces for a less candid purpose. If the authority does stop Anonymia from enlarging its forces, Anonymia may undergo a revolution, or fall apart.)

The present tenuous beginnings of a vague consensus of acceptance of international authority are a long way from that kind of world order. This is still a very nationalist world; some of its nationalisms are still on the increase. The consensus has begun to grow, and is likely to go on growing, in a lumpy, sporadic, often haphazard way as the nations stagger into one crisis after another, and each moment of general alarm provides an opportunity for enlarging the competence of the UN.

Many praiseworthy attempts to draw up blueprints for a workable world order have already been made, and there is every reason to go on studying the essential principles of such an order, despite all the glaring difficulties of putting them into practice. But our chances of ever escaping from the nuclear rat-race, and reaching the disarmed and peaceful world which is the dream of all peoples and the declared goal of all their governments, do not depend on blueprints. They must depend most of all on our making the means of international peace-keeping that we already have more effective.

To do that, we have to overcome our split-mindedness about the United Nations. To gain in effectiveness, it needs more than improved procedures and physical equipment. It needs a readier acceptance of its role as (in Hammarskjöld's phrase) 'a dynamic instrument' for resolving conflicts, or, better still, averting them. This acceptance, in turn, can come only when politicians and public alike shed their present illusions about the UN, and see its achievements, shortcomings, and potentialities for what they are. Thus, one of the very first steps along the road to a peaceful world must be an advance to a better understanding of what has really happened, and is still happening, in the dimly seen evolution of the United Nations.

Suggested Reading

As well as the books listed below, there are, of course, the official publications of the United Nations itself; inquiries about these may be made at the UN Information Centre in London (14 Stratford Place, W1). There are also the publications issued independently by the United Nations Association (25 Charles Street, London W1) in Britain and by similar associations in other countries.

Sydney D. Bailey, *The General Assembly of the United Nations*, Stevens, London, and Praeger, New York, 1960.

Sydney D. Bailey, *The Secretariat of the United Nations*, Carnegie Endowment, New York, 1962.

Lincoln P. Bloomfield, *The United Nations and U.S. Foreign Policy*, Little, Brown, Boston and Toronto, 1960.

Viscount Cecil (Lord Robert Cecil), *A Great Experiment*, Cape, London, 1941.

Alexander Dallin, *The Soviet Union at the United Nations*, Praeger, New York, 1962.

William R. Frye, *A United Nations Peace Force*, Stevens, London, and Oceana, New York, 1957.

Arthur L. Gavshon, *The Mysterious Death of Dag Hammarskjöld*, Walker, New York, and McLeod, Toronto, 1962; and, as *The Last Days of Dag Hammarskjöld*, Barrie and Rockcliff, London, 1963.

Geoffrey L. Goodwin, *Britain and the United Nations*, Oxford University Press, 1957.

John Hadwen and Johan Kaufmann, *How United Nations Decisions are Made*, Sythoff, Leyden, and Oceana, New York, 1960; revised edition 1962.

Joseph P. Lash, *Dag Hammarskjöld*, Doubleday, New York, 1961; Cassell, London, 1962.

Trygve Lie, *In the Cause of Peace*, Macmillan, London, 1954.

Andrew Martin and John B. S. Edwards, *The Changing Charter*, Sylvan Press, London, 1955.

Bernard Moore, *The Second Lesson*, Macmillan, London, 1957.

H. G. Nicholas, *The United Nations as a Political Institution*, Oxford University Press, 1959; revised edition, paperback, O.U.P., 1962.

Conor Cruise O'Brien, *To Katanga and Back*, Hutchinson, London 1962, and Simon and Schuster, New York, 1963.

Stephen M. Schwebel, *The Secretary-General of the United Nations*, Harvard University Press and Oxford University Press, 1952.

Index

Index

*Some more Penguin
publications are described
on the following pages*

A PELICAN BOOK

VOTERS, PARTIES, AND LEADERS
The Social Fabric of British Politics

Jean Blondel

Are we witnessing the end of class-barriers in the political behaviour of the British voter? Does the businessman vote like the railwayman, the white-collar worker like the un-skilled labourer?

Of course they do not. But how different are their voting habits? Trade Unions are Labour-inclined, but all trade unionists are not Labour men. Are these non-Labour trade unionists exceptional? And, at the other end of the scale, are Labour-inclined professional people, managers, and executives rare but interesting exceptions?

These are some of the questions which the newly ap-pointed Professor of Government in the University of Essex attempts to answer in this original book. In examining the background, outlook, and interests of voters, party members, politicians, civil servants, and party leaders, and endeavouring to trace some of the subtle threads that tie certain individuals to certain organizations, he presents an anatomy of the political world. And he asks: 'What is the "Establishment" we talk of? Does it exist? And if so, does it rule?'

A PELICAN BOOK

THE CONSUMER, SOCIETY AND THE LAW

Gordon Borrie and Aubrey L. Diamond

'It may be a cherished adage of the consuming public that the customer is always right, but in the eyes of the law this saying has never been significant.'

From the opening pages of *The Consumer, Society and the Law* we are at the heart of the Consumer Movement. Here for the first time is an authoritative survey of the whole area in which, as customer and consumer, John Citizen meets the law.

We sign HP agreements, have furniture repaired, take clothes to the laundry, order food in restaurants, book up holidays, open bank accounts, take out insurance policies, buy tickets to travel ... but we seldom understand the law that covers the transaction until it is too late.

This new Pelican provides the only complete guide to the customer's rights and obligations. It deals, moreover, with restrictive practices, monopoly, and price maintenance. Setting each topic in its social and historical context it explains what the law is, why it is what it is, and whether, for our present society, it is enough.

A PELICAN BOOK

FREEDOM, THE INDIVIDUAL AND THE LAW

Harry Street

Civil Liberties are very much in the news. At the heart of every incident that concerns the rights and obligations of the individual lies a conflict, sometimes muted, sometimes violent, between competing interests: freedom of speech *v.* security of the state, freedom of movement *v.* public order, the right to privacy *v.* professional integrity. Every day brings fresh reports of 'punch-up' politics, banning of controversial posters, curious corners of theatre censorship, abuse of telephone tapping, contempt of Parliament ... the headlines never stop.

Yet Professor Street's *Freedom, the Individual and the Law* is the first comprehensive survey of the way English law deals with the many sides of Civil Liberty. After an introductory description of the powers of the police, Professor Street addresses himself in detail to the main areas of freedom of expression, freedom of association, and freedom of movement. Protection against private power, the right to work, and other subjects of contemporary importance make up the citizen's first guide to the theory and practice of Civil Liberty.

A PELICAN BOOK

THE FAMILY AND THE LAW
The Law of Marriage, Separation, and Divorce

Margaret Puxon

In *The Family and the Law* Margaret Puxon, who uniquely combines the roles of mother, doctor, and barrister, ranges over the social and legal realities of many topics from the formalities of getting married, separation, maintenance, divorce, cruelty, and domicile to the whole area of the law as it affects the child, both as a member of the family and as part of the State's responsibility.

Here, in short, is a complete picture of the law relating to the family as it stands today.

A PELICAN BOOK

IN DEFENCE OF POLITICS

Bernard Crick

'One of the most thoughtful products of the political dialogues of the London School of Economics since the great days of Tawney, Dalton, Wallas, and Hobhouse. Its sobriety, liberal spirit, and toughness of mind are rare qualities in any political work' – *Guardian*

At a time of brittle cynicism about the activities of politicians, this essay makes 'an attempt to justify politics in plain words by saying what it is'. In a civilized community, which is no mere tribe, the establishment among rival groups and interests of political order – of agreed rules for the game – marks the birth of freedom. In spite of the compromises, deals, half-measures, and bargains which prompt impatient idealists to regard politics as a dirty word – indeed, because of them – the negotiating processes of politics remain the only tested alternative to government by outright coercion.

'Original and profound. It is hard to think of anyone interested in politics at any level who would not benefit by reading it' – Max Beloff in the *Daily Telegraph*

TRAFFIC IN TOWNS

The specially shortened edition of the Buchanan Report

'We are nourishing a monster of great potential destructiveness.'

The motor car is the menace that prompted Professor Colin Buchanan's famous report, *Traffic in Towns*. This is the most comprehensive, objective, and radical examination of urban traffic and its effect on the conditions of urban living that has ever been made.

Because of its profuse illustrations the H.M.S.O. edition of *Traffic in Towns* had necessarily to be published at £2 10s. This Penguin edition is a condensation which has been approved by Professor Buchanan and which omits none of the main arguments or conclusions of the report. It permits this important document to appear at a price which will enable a very much wider public to comprehend the gigantic and terrifyingly urgent task with which Britain is now faced.